Stardust Awakens

From Social Isolation to Finding Your Purpose and Destiny

Rev Dr Joseph Randolph Bowers

Ability Therapy Specialists Pty Ltd

Stardust Awakens

Publication

Stardust Awakens: From Social Isolation to Finding Your Purpose and Destiny © 2020 Joseph Randolph Bowers. Cover Image © 2020 Dr Dwayne Andrew Kennedy. All rights reserved. No part of this publication may be reproduced, stored in a retrieval system, or transmitted in any form or by any means electronic or mechanical, photocopying, recording or otherwise, without the express written permission of the publisher. Ability Therapy Specialists Pty Ltd, PO Box 4065, Armidale, New South Wales, Australia 2350, www.abilitytherapyspecialists.com.au.
ISBN: 978-1-925034-06-6
First Edition (2013) under the title: 'On the Threshold: Personal Transformation and Spiritual Awakening'
Keywords: Personal growth, development, spirituality, mysticism, self-help, empowerment, healing, awaken, consciousness, old soul, Native, Indigenous, First Nation, Aboriginal, Celtic, Druid, western, psychology, counselling, psychotherapy, education, life-long, change, learning, capacity, ceremony, ritual, journaling, reflection, retreat, solitude.
Disclaimer: This book is for entertainment purposes only and is not an authoritative source of information. Readers ought to seek direct medical advice as your authoritative source of information. Do not rely on what you read in this book or elsewhere, do your research, and consult with your medical practitioner. The publisher makes no representations or warranties as to the accuracy or completeness of the information contained in this book. The publisher disclaims all liability for all claims, expenses, losses, damages and costs any person may incur as a result of the information contained in this publication, for any reason, being inaccurate, or incomplete in any way or incapable or achieving any purpose. These statements do not disclaim statutory obligations as deemed necessary under the law.

Joseph Randolph Bowers

About this Book

A guidebook for the soul. Learn to develop your spiritual strengths. Activate your experiential learning. Integrate your knowledge into practice. An experiential eightfold path follows the sacred wisdom of native and western mysticism. Learn hidden secrets of personal potential and spiritual power. Actively become conscious. Make decisions about growth and life. Regain the spirit of youth. Enkindle the Elder. Acknowledge personal strength. Attend to weakness with compassion. Come to terms with identity and place. Exercise pathwork to discover inner purpose. Define transformation. Come to terms with destiny. With over thirty-five years of intensive searching, the author shares many ancient secrets of the mystical life woven into a modern and balanced psychology. Now in second edition. Completely accessible. Profoundly life changing for people new to personal growth. Inspiring. A touchstone for those further along the path of enlightenment.

About the Author

Rev Dr Joseph Randolph Bowers is a Senior Clinical Behaviour Specialist Counsellor Psychotherapist with Ability Therapy Specialists Pty Ltd. His formal qualifications include a PhD, MEd Couns, Grad Cert Higher Edu, BA Distinction, CPNLP, HACA. Dr Bowers is an Honorary of the Australian Counselling Association, co-founder of the Australian Counselling Research Journal, and among the founders of the Psychotherapy and Counselling Federation of Australia. Rev Dr Bowers is an ordained minister in the independent apostolic movement, and Honorary Recipient of the Eagle Feather from Mi'kmaq First Nation Elders in Sacred Council; an Associate Scholar with the Centre for World Indigenous Studies, and member of Spiritual Directors International. An author of over 200 works, books include: The Practice of Counselling; Sacred Teachings from the Medicine Lodge; Mi'kmaq Puoinaq Two Spirit Medicine; Solitude Awakens: The Heart, Forest, Mountain Way; Mass of Creation: Liturgies and Prayers for All Occasions.

Joseph Randolph Bowers

Reader's Comments

- A narrative reflection on spiritual meaning in daily life.
- A gifted writer and storyteller.
- Openly discusses challenges, struggles, and insights.
- Compelling prose.
- A reminder of the importance in honouring culture.
- Highlighting the sacredness of the earth.
- Teaching the critical importance of emotional and spiritual wholeness.
- A must read for mental health professionals.
- Important for religious leaders interested in understanding the nexus between western psychotherapy, indigenous healing, and mysticism.
- An important resource.
- A valuable read to help us reaffirm family and friends.
- Puts technology, material things, and a busy life in their place.
- Provides solid direction to keep on track with your chosen values and beliefs.
- Your window to growing in self-awareness.
- One of the most unique thinkers in the contemporary counselling world.
- A window into a counsellor's life journey.
- A work that illustrates vividly how an individual can use personal experiences, including negative events and mistakes, to grow into a more contented and productive human being.
- The author demonstrates a receptive mind and that he has learned many lessons well.

More Reader's Comments

- A guide to reflect on our lives as professional counsellors and citizens of our planet.
- A clear, concise treatment of a rather complex subject.
- Very good for self-study, or in a group.
- Valuable to anyone who is honestly seeking meaning in life.
- With this book as a guide, you will be sure to get back tenfold the energy and time you put into this journey.
- This book is meant to be so that others can find their path and understand when they are on the right path.
- I am inspired to revisit the journey of my past and the journey I have yet to take.
- As this book says, our path is about honouring Spirit, the Old People, the Elders, our Ancestor's and the ones who are yet to come.
- Important reading to find your place in life and to understand your purpose as family members, helpers, healers, and counsellors.
- A story about how to go about a life-long search for meaning with the many obstacles that can stand in the way.
- Dr Bowers searched for meaning in many different places, only to realize that the truth resides within.
- This book opens your path to your own way in life. This is about honouring the Spirit within; while learning about and honouring and respect of life.
- The author rightly states that the search to find ourselves and establish our identity is a task that only each individual can pursue.

More Reader's Comments

- The author is courageous in telling his own story.
- An inspiring book that helps one learn how to live an authentic and fulfilling life.
- Unearths a discovery of one's spiritual identity – a truly extraordinary journey.
- We learn that society obstructs our connection and safe passage to enlightenment.
- Visionary guidance shared in these pages reveals a path to meaning, serenity, and peace.
- Dr Bowers is straightforward and truthful.
- Rev Dr Bowers speaks to genuineness, spiritual awakening, and the transformation of an individual's strengths and hopes.
- This is a unique and remarkable book about survival and endurance, written with compassion, providing vital links to spirituality and humanity.
- Rev Dr Bowers has an awareness that arises from living a life-quest for knowledge in the forefront, and he is using his wisdom wisely.
- Thought provoking and a must read.
- Provides deep insight into the inner self and raises questions about the meaning of life and the unity of nature and spirituality.
- He contends that wisdom today has been forgotten and needs to be regained, renewed, and revived to meet the challenges of the modern age.
- The author points to the need to be attuned with the core intentions of the Creator so our unique gifts can help others.
- A feast for thought!

Dedication

To our late father and grandmother and to a long line of French Acadian and Mi'kmaq First Nation hero-warriors going back to 1652 with the arrival of Michel Richard in the colony of Acadia, a community founded in the enduring relations of marriage between two nations in mutual respect, upon the esteemed territories of the Mi'kmaq Nation.

To our mother for her steadiness, love of reading, and her spiritual wisdom; and to our Celtic heritage in the deep forest of the Old World of Bards, Ovates, and Druids who inspired the evolution of western mysticism through the ages.

To our Australian Aboriginal family, and to the Dreaming.

To the Old Law, living still in Rock, Stone, and Tree...

This book is dedicated to the Awakening.
M'sit No'koma, Ta'ho

Acknowledgements

This work celebrates well over thirty-five years of practice, learning, and testing the teachings that inspire personal growth. It is difficult to offer adequate thanks to so many who have instructed and guided along this path. Regardless, we must pay forward some respect.

Friends and mentors, Fr Basil Pennington OCSO, Fr Peter Vasko OFM, Fr Phil Thibodeau, Sister Vivian McKenna SC, Redge Craig, Most Reverend Bishop Ronald W. Langham DD, Most Reverend Peter Johnson, Brother Fr Luke Koller EFO, Brother Fr Simeon EFO, Chief Frank Meuse, and Elders Georgina Doucette, Lottie Johnson, Grace and John Kennedy, Janet and Roy Edmonds, Diane and Frank Roberts.

Esteemed colleagues, Professors Judy Atkinson, Marie Battiste, Ron Chenail, Irene Coulson, James A. Foster, Lynda Garland, Kathryn Geldard, Jacques Goulet, Kay Harman, Arthur (Andy) Horne, Lyn Irwin, Diane Janes, Jeffrey Kottler, Jeanne Madison, Rodrigo Marino, Cathryn McConaghy, Phil McShane, Victor Minichiello, Patrick O'Brien, Ina Olahan, Susan O'Loughlan, Nadine Pelling, David Plummer, Rudolph C. Ryser, Brian Sullivan, John Sumarah, Catherine Sun, and esteemed colleagues Philip Armstrong, Diane Chisholm, Ann Denny, Lindsay Marshall, Chief Phil Fontaine, Jane Lewis, and Wanda Muise. Also to highly regarded students, post-graduate and doctoral research students, clinical supervisees, colleagues-in-practice, and clients near and far ~ thank you for inspiring us to continue this work. Without your feedback and guidance, we could not have come this far.

Beloved and cherished family Dwayne Andrew, Dennis, Lisa, David, Kay, Denny, Donna, and Jonna Kennedy; Joseph and Jeanette Bowers; Betty, Charlie, Jon, Josh and Emily Ritchie; Angela, Brian, Erica and Kyle Rudolph; Tommy Edgecombe, Sherri Saunders-Carty, Annette Leblanc-Power, Joe Bergeron, Sonja Bruggeman, Bernice, Jenny, and Daniel Doucette; Catherine-Ann and Mac Fuller, Reg Gibson, Ellen Hunt, James Jeremy, Rose and Nathan Muise-Waterman, Gloria and Richard Wood.

Sacred Guides and Custodians. Four legged companions. Honoured trees and sacred grove. Fire-pit and nights under stars. Eastern Door and Eagle Medicine of Turtle Island. Southern Door and Sacred Gums of Gondwana Land ~ no acknowledgement is enough.

Table of Contents

Publication	2
About this Book	3
About the Author	4
Reader's Comments	5
More Reader's Comments	6
More Reader's Comments	7
Dedication	8
Acknowledgements	9
Table of Contents	11
Preface	13
Our Approach	14
Sacred Medicine Traditions	16
Thresholds Awaken	19
Spirituality and Psychotherapy	21
Integral Holistic Methods	24
Experiential Learning	27
Methods of Self Awareness	31
Identity Crisis and Healing	34
Habits of Thought	36
Reconnecting	39
No One is an Island	41
How to Read this Book	42
My Spiritual Agreement	46
1 Ground: Between the Worlds	49
Activity 1 Personal Story	79

2 East: Threshold of Manifestation	**82**
Activity 2:1 Keeping a Journal	*105*
Activity 2:2 Meditation Practice	*106*
3 South: Activating Spiritual Potential	**108**
Activity 3:1 Examination of Conscience	*121*
Activity 3:2 Inventory of Daily Life	*122*
Activity 3:3 Dream List for the Future	*122*
4 West: Making a Dream Catcher	**124**
Activity 4:1 Collecting Stones	*142*
Activity 4:2 Opening the Sacred Circle	*147*
Activity 4:3 Reclaiming Personal Space	*150*
5 North: Youth Will See Visions	**153**
Activity 5 Personal Retreat as Self-care	*166*
6 Above: Personal Transformation	**171**
Activity 6 Intuitive Awakening	*193*
7 Below: Healing Yourself and Others	**196**
Activity 7:1 Ten Minute Spirit Meditation	*206*
Activity 7:2 Spirit Walk	*207*
8 Centre: Power to Change the World	**208**
Activity 8 Manifesting, Empowering	*226*
Conclusion	**233**
Activity 9 Stardust Awakening	*241*

Preface

This book began with a spiritual vision that came during a time of physical and psychological crisis. In constant physical pain that manifested in muscle and neurological systems, the crisis followed several years of intensive struggles to grow and learn. At the same time, we were doing work that opened our body-mind to new possibilities; and during that time, we even finished a graduate degree in psychotherapy. It felt like our core identity was being tested to the limit. The psyche was stretched beyond what we could readily deal with. Beneath all of this external work and social engagement, a deep sense of shame drove us to cover-up our identity and what was happening. Like most males in this society, we had become expert at concealing any signs of vulnerability.

In the midst of this time, denial of our identity led to using psychotherapeutic skills to change cognition and thought patterns within identity. For a time, we were successful in changing identity. But this generated a false calm before an even larger storm. The longer we maintained this lie, the more we suffered.

The enormous psychological, emotional, and spiritual stress created an opening in the psyche. The result was that even while facing chronic fatigue and hopelessness, spiritual visions arose within us that would guide and direct our life for years to come. It was this paradox – the combination of suffering with the giftedness of spiritual insight – that led to writing this book.

This experience taught me that suffering in humanity hides and holds many obscured keys to an arduous passage into the spiritual realms. The path involves very real risk to health and safety, as well as symbolic and metaphorical dimensions of life and death. There are significant gateways and thresholds between humanity and spiritual power. These must be travelled at your own risk; and with an honest heart. When you walk with integrity, you will open the gates of true identity. But to pass through this experience and to survive the challenges that you will meet along the way takes an enormous amount of courage.

For many people these awakenings take a lifetime and do not blossom in personal awareness until later in life. For others spiritual gateways open very quickly and cause great disruption to normal everyday life. And for those who are born old spirits or simply are gifted beyond the scope of most of us, spiritual power comes easily but is harnessed and directed only through many sacrifices.

From the suffering of the past, the visions given opened many insights. But that was not the end. It was only the beginning. Over three decades had to pass before the energy of life made this book possible to complete. Over those years the profound spiritual inspiration that was given in youth was tested, tried, and found worthy of commitment to writing. Ancient is this story and very modern. Today more than ever we need trusted insight that arise from these primordial springs.

Our Approach

However instead of giving you the standard line on personal development that is based in the literature of western psychology, this approach is unique. Although our work includes senior scholarship and leadership in our fields of practice, this is not good enough. Professional language and frameworks do not speak adequately to the depth of human development. You and the rest of society deserve more than western scholarship and science have to offer at this time.

Indeed, the western academe has strayed from its original intentions that began during the middle Ages, when the purpose of western science was to open the gates of human insight, knowledge, and wisdom. The ultimate aim of the early founders was to facilitate personal and spiritual transformation. Much of the roots of philosophy and science are based in the spirituality and mysticism of the west. It is terribly ironic that today these original intentions of the academe are subverted by what are surely passing trends based in empirical materialism.

But real life sees people in the everyday world facing issues that need more than modern education can provide. As a counselling psychotherapist, healer, traditional medicine keeper, and minister of the spirit, many people have sought us for help with issues they never learned about in school or university. Life today causes huge challenges, many defeats, even more mistakes, and often leads to identity crisis instead of spiritual enlightenment. People today are facing survival of terrible circumstances. And even more ironic is the fact that the wealth of western knowledge, insight, and wisdom remains essentially hidden from view.

Our effort over the past few decades was to practice the arts and sciences of spirituality and mysticism while engaging in continual study and work. As the spirit underwent a process of awakening in-body, this pathwork enabled the entity within to remember its true identity and purpose. Eventually the quest led us to seek beyond the western academe and to explore the sacred worlds of familial connections within Aboriginal Dreaming and

First Nation Medicine traditions; and in the ancient Celtic and Druidic traditions. These more recent studies and experiential pathways in mysticism follow extensive work within the lesser-known Franciscan, mendicant, monastic, and eremitic desert paths of western and eastern Christian mystical teachings.

Understanding that this manuscript was first written between 2010 and was first published during 2013, the information here predates other work that we have done since. For instance, about a year before completing this manuscript revision as a second edition of the book that was titled 'On the Threshold,' during 2019, we published the book 'Solitude Awakens: The Heart Forest Mountain Way.' This project expressed the ongoing journey into deep spiritual agreements and vowed living that in many ways begins here in this book.

While an aside, you might like to know that during 2014, we almost died from cardiomyopathy. At the time, the publishing efforts that had been made were suspended. Due to government and corporate policies, while recovering we had to stop work for a full year and this necessitated closure of publishing projects and pulling books from distribution. The book that existed in first edition was only available in press for less than a year and was permanently withdrawn. As such, while this edition is revised and updated, and was subjected to a comprehensive editing process, in many respects we feel this manuscript is the first of its kind. In any case, we see this as the second edition of On the Threshold.

Sacred Medicine Traditions

Thus, in a symbolic way I would like to invite you into the 'Medicine Lodge.' The Medicine Wigwam is a place that is quite intimate. A personal lodge is circular and only about ten feet wide at the base with a fire pit in the middle. Another word for wigwam is tipi, and while most people can stand tall inside the space, one must bend low to enter the Eastern Door of the Lodge. You will find that we use capital letters when using words in a sacred manner, an approach that gently shifts awareness into a sense of reverence and respect. Also, in this Medicine Lodge we will use many words to describe the energy of life, evolution, and spirituality. We take these words to hold important metaphors that inspire different ways of understanding divine life and spiritual meaning. Words like God, Goddess, Creator, Great Spirit, Life, Energy of Evolution, Higher Power etc., express only a tiny window into the Great Mystery.

At another level, as we explain within this book, we do not define these words per se, nor do we suggest any one theology because the focus here is on encouraging each person to resonate with the ideas that are shared and to explore the mystery of life and meaning for yourself. Prior knowledge, belief or faith are not required to read this book. Agnostics and atheists are just as welcome here. Indeed, we consider our path as an agnostic in as much as the word means 'one who is uncertain' and 'seeker of truth.' Indeed, the nature of questions and uncertain searching is a lauded native way of life. By comparison to set theology, doctrine, and religion this more flexible experiential approach tends to be healthier and more creative. This path walks between faith and doubt.

In this Wigwam, we share stories around the Sacred Fire. The word 'wigwam' in traditional Mi'kmaq First Nation language means 'place of family.' The image of the wigwam provides a strand of cultural meaning that guides this book in a gentle way. In this cultural space we are not bound by the dictates of western methods. At the same time, we pay respect where respect is due. In being real with you in this manner we do not want to hide behind professional status even though we have paid our dues in the land of degrees, western scholarship, professional teaching, and many years of clinical practice. Instead, we can share a common humanity and through our stories we can find spiritual medicine for health, wellness, balance, and beauty.

We may face individual crisis at specific times along our journey and we may take long periods of time to heal from our wounds, but in the bigger picture we are not quite human and not quite divine. In spite of ourselves and without warning we find that we are caught within this in-between state. Only a gift of wisdom can tell us that we are on the journey to becoming a divine being. This threshold holds great potential. We can understand this purely from a developmental perspective, although these words imply much more.

During each stage along our journey to maturity we human beings, step into a new thresholds of growth and potential. At each turn we have many choices to make that over time come to define who we are. Particularly as we become adults and leave the world of youth behind, our choices will determine if we push through and grow or if we will lose hope. There are other alternatives. Many people throughout history and in the present day have had to dig deep inside themselves to find a source of hope. We must remember that the purpose of hope is to see beyond all the struggles and pain that exist in today's world. Hope is not an idle wish. Hope is an essential function of the human spirit and psyche.

Taking the path towards becoming a more fully mature and actualised human being is not easy and demands many sacrifices. It is not easy to go against the status quo and to challenge the essence of values and beliefs that define our corporate and political world. To make your life a sign and symbol of something more real may not be an easy process but is a goal worth attaining. During these efforts hope provides a ray of light – but imagine being able to tap into the source of hope and the ancient wellsprings of creation from which all light comes. This is where we seek to be.

What we are discussing in this book cuts to the core of what it means to be human. This is not about creating a peaceful spiritual revolution; it is about acknowledging a pervasive spiritual evolution that is already taking place at the heart of humanity. And evolution is far from peaceful. During evolutionary history whole species have gone extinct. Life and death dance together during the cycles of manifestation of creative energy. We can only resist our true identity at our own peril. By saying this I am not striking a fearful blow at the heart of humanity but only suggesting that the spiritual evolution of our species involves the elemental forces of life and death. And once we are even slightly aware of this we cannot easily turn back. The awareness we gain carries its own momentum and opens new pathways that become inextricably linked to our personal destiny.

Thresholds Awaken

From a larger perspective the struggles and worries of everyday life and indeed, the greatest hardships and setbacks of human history are all steppingstones toward the ongoing creation of loving, compassionate and spiritually gifted human beings. The stages that stand between normal human beings and more evolved, spiritually powerful beings are the thresholds of manifestation. Within each of these thresholds we manifest abilities to nurture, sustain, govern, and heal ourselves within the energies of creation. There are shadow thresholds that manifest from desires to control, influence, dominate, and press personal ego-identity into self-serving manifestations. The choice to take the path of peace can sometimes take even more courage and commitment because this path suggests values of altruism, selflessness, and giving more than we receive.

Many prophets and poets have invited ordinary people to see and experience the extraordinary. Even during the darkest hours of human actions, this possibility of taking a higher road to human excellence shines forth. The visions that were given to me in my past came from this higher transpersonal perspective on human history. We believe these visions were not given merely for individual enlightenment. Although the messages received inspired and directed our life, the insights were not meant for personal gain. Indeed, they have cost me much during the learning processes that followed and that ultimately led to this time of sharing these lessons with you.

During the deepest darkness, when we lost hope the most, the idea of sharing this wisdom with you kept me going. How we are connected helped me to survive social upheaval, loss and grief, years of darkness and depression, and very many sacrifices of family, country, and nation to travel around the world when this journey demanded that we keep going. We learned that as much as we are created as members of a family, tribe, and nation; our spiritual calling can sometimes demand everything. As spirit-entity beings having a human experience in-body and in-relationship, the first part of our lives is about finding our meaning in life. The rest of our lives is about living our purpose. But to find both meaning and purpose, our identity needs to be clarified and purified, confusion reduced, and trauma resolved. That spells a lot of work for most of us! But then, from the clean spirit-entity within, as if arising from the ashes, our soulful mindfulness awakens to meaning-finding and meaning-sorting that had all occurred during our vision questing years of youth. We spiral back upon what was, and that is suddenly made new.

What we have learned since the days of vision quest is that the threshold awakening philosophy has been developed across the centuries and in different cultures. There is little that is in fact new under the sun. Although there is much that has been forgotten and needs to be regained, renewed, reconnected, and revived. What is new and unique to this presentation is how the various pieces of the picture are brought together and applied to a contemporary perspective on human growth. This is the central task of every generation – to articulate the meaning and purpose of human life in ways that make sense for today.

Spirituality and Psychotherapy

In this regard, several people have asked, how does this holistic and spiritual perspective relate to modern professions that are steeped in empirical materialism, humanism, and largely coded and set ways of working? How does this 'threshold awakens' philosophy sit next to medicine, psychology, counselling, and social work?

The emphasis on spirituality and spiritual phenomena sits extremely well and works seamlessly within a well-formed western and contemporary professional and scholarly perspective. For many today this is not the case. Because modern practice across the professions has deleted classical education in the arts and humanities as the basis for entry into professional training programs. The majority of practitioners today lack a culture of wisdom and its associated frameworks for understanding complex phenomena. This coupled with the dominant beliefs and values of the day that are based mainly in empirical materialism means that people have great difficulty in understanding holistic and spiritual phenomena.

For example, the pervasive approach to dealing with spiritual phenomena across the fields of psychiatry, psychology, clinical counselling, and allied fields such as nursing, social work, and the human services disciplines is to frame people's visions, spiritual crisis, and awakening processes as well as people's capacity for heightened sensory awareness as forms of dysfunction, emotional trauma, mental illness, and psychosis.

On one hand, contemporary professional perspectives need to become more holistic and open to traditional cultural beliefs that allow for vision and a degree of personal crisis, because in the wider view these experiences open pathways to transformation of the person. Indeed, what most people actually need is consistent and loving support that creates safety during times of spiritual crisis and awakening. This presents great challenges for professions whose daily approach is based in diagnostic assessment frameworks focused on curing or treating problems.

On the other hand, traditional cultural perspectives may at times resist out of hand the mainstream western treatment regimes. This poses challenges for people with more holistic cultural and spiritual ways of understanding. It can equally be true that many traditional cultural approaches acknowledge that people may need additional help and support through modern medical and psychological interventions including psychotropic drugs and/or psychotherapy.

While these two contexts are concerning, there is another quite common issue that needs to be addressed and that forms the main focus of this book. People today do not possess a way of making sense and meaning of the natural processes of growth, awakening, and coming into their true identity. When not properly understood, appreciated, and supported these emotional, psychological, and spiritual experiences tend to be treated as problems to be solved by medical or psychological means. In every case, regardless how extreme, medical and psychological advice is warranted and always advised. However, in many cases it would be very helpful to understand that the natural processes of growth and identity development require a holistic knowledge and appreciation.

More to the point, we acknowledge that spiritual visions and psychic phenomena can tend to occur during times of depression, anxiety, and great personal challenges. There are several ways to read this context. Under medical models we might treat the experience as a disruption to daily life and normal functioning. In these cases, many practitioners tend to consider a temporary adjustment disorder that will pass with time. Psychotherapy may be recommended. If the disruption continues more than six months, people may begin to consider other forms of illness depending on the symptoms.

In contrasting approaches, a counselling psychotherapist may consider an empathic appreciation for the individual's coping strategies, capacities for emotional awareness, and ability to address the deeper relational issues associated with life transitions. For example, the person's context in terms of challenges at work, home, and with major developmental issues may be considered as significant and as contributing to the emotional and spiritual 'disturbance.' Likewise, a holistic practitioner may consider other possibilities depending on their emphasis, training, and philosophy.

In many ways the interpretation and approach to helping is dependent on the strengths, abilities, and limitations of the practitioner as well as the beliefs, values, and expectations of the person seeking assistance. Human experience is contextual, and our understanding is limited. At the best of times our perspective is opened up through sharing perspectives. But if this process is limited to people who do not have wider views and an awareness of other possibilities, the outcome can still remain entirely limiting. This is why continual learning, education, and training is so important. But more so, why very many so-called alternative practitioners tend to exist precisely because their personal experiences of growth have outstretched the boundaries of most modern western empirical and materialistic cartesian restrictions.

Integral Holistic Methods

Because there is so much written about the first two models noted above, allow me to speak to the holistic perspective. Initially it may help to understand that most holistic perspectives appear outwardly simple and elegant. Holistic models tend to be based in cultural forms of meaning that see connections, synergies, and patterns.

In fact, the more you learn about integral holistic methods the more you begin to see they are quite complex and tend toward using maps and systems that trace patterns of interactions and inter-relationships. From this perspective we can read depression, anxiety, and various forms of personality and identity crisis including the more complex spiritual phenomena as processes that are related to intra-psychic and relational contexts. With a more holistic appreciation for these processes, we know that in many cases profound openings of the psyche can enable spiritual transformation or conversely, suggest either temporary or more enduring forms of emotional and psychological challenges.

For example, during times of great personal stress, like facing the death of a loved one, a person can experience the opening of spiritual doorways to vision and psychic phenomena that are difficult to understand when these experiences appear to come out of the blue. However, for others who accept such experiences as part of a cultural way of understanding, these difficult transitions may be a bit easier because the information that comes forward through spiritual insight might be more readily available.

There are many stories of people seeing their deceased loved one or of happening upon a bird or other creature felt to be a messenger or manifestation of the loved one who is passed over. Others intuitively know what their children or partner is going through when separated by great distances. Many people experience deeper connections to the environment and ecology around them during times of personal crisis, when they may turn inward for strength while seeking solace in nature. From these experiences people often grow enormously, having received spiritual insight and guidance that informs their life for years to come. The key idea is that instead of assuming these experiences are forms of illness, by providing consistent and loving support and by attending the deeper meaning and purpose of these experiences we can allow ourselves to slowly integrate spiritual awakening into our personality.

In traditional Native contexts even though spiritual ways of knowing are integral to the culture, spiritual visions rarely if ever come with a training manual. People tend to expect to not know the meaning of visions, and a great deal of humour is associated with being dumfounded by the many mysteries of life. The reality is that spiritual vision demands that we stay open to the many ways of viewing the experience. Meaning comes to us over time. But the first test for us is usually patience combined with nurturing a listening heart.

People in First Nation cultures learn to stay open and listen, to observe, and to give lots of time for insight to come forward. In mainstream systems we can use these kinds of attitudes and skills of attending to spiritual and psychic phenomena to help people in more holistic ways. Likewise, in extreme and long-term circumstances there are situations when mental illness becomes psychosis and needs to be treated by modern medicine and psychiatry. I would suggest that even in these circumstances and alongside of medical and psychological interventions we can benefit by using a holistic model that provides person centred support while taking medication and undergoing psychotherapy.

This focus on spiritual emergence as a problem to be solved takes up a great deal of time and energy for many people. It is therefore quite important to shift the focus a bit and come to terms with spiritual awakening as a process in and of itself. What does spiritual awakening mean? What are the parts of this process? How can we help people to understand and appreciate their spiritual growth experiences?

Experiential Learning

Throughout this discussion we will look at the nature of spiritual awakening, but our focus will not be about passing on intellectual information. Rather, the focus of this book is experiential. We wish to explore personal transformation by engaging processes of listening, learning, and gaining self-awareness. We will investigate the parts of the process of spiritual awakening and provide you with examples and ways to practice that promote growth and learning. In a quite general way, by gaining this knowledge combined by the wisdom that comes from your personal practice, you may come to appreciate spiritual insights and perhaps become a bit more open during the difficult transitions of life.

Spiritual life is not all about coping and dealing with difficulties. By far the greatest and most exciting aspects of spiritual awakening relate to growth in human potential and living the manifest divine life on earth. These processes are about being the best person you can be. Being happy. Nurturing contentment. Finding and keeping an abiding sense of peace and wellness. Living a life of deeper compassion, and living in forgiveness, acceptance, and loving kindness.

Spiritual awakening is also about putting the difficult parts of life into a much more holistic and resourceful picture that is based in the powerful nature of the human spirit - and what it really means to be a spiritual being in the wider contexts and relationships that we can have within the world around us and within the ecology and the cosmos. By coming to terms with the widest scope of potentials and possibilities that spiritual awakening represents, you may find yourself quite surprised by how joyful and wonderful your life has become.

Over the centuries, poets, saints, and philosophers have said that we are the manifestation of the Creator on this earth. From an even more grounded and Indigenous perspective there is no need to distinguish between the identities of human beings and the Creator. We are all one, in one great Circle of Life. And yet we are Many.

From an appreciation for the spirituality of evolution and ecology we know that Mother Earth is a living, breathing, and feeling Being. We actually live in a world of great spiritual mystery and wonder. From a personal view it is hard to imagine why and how people have lost this vital perspective. Acknowledging the wonder and mystery of life is an essential element in human belief systems and psychological health that allows us to form relationships of respect for the world around us. These patterns of feeling and thought allow human beings to form better coping strategies that include forming values, systems of ethics, and moral codes that assist us in maintaining healthy relationships and that give us ways to protect the environment from generation to generation.

Western forms of empirical materialism have coincided with values inherent in the industrial and now technological revolutions that encourage disconnection and lack of wonder and mystery. Industry and technology can be integrated into holistic ways of living. It is only logical to acknowledge that the longer we maintain systems and practices that go against the flow of life, the more we increase the chances of our own extinction.

On the spiritual level, our evolution demands becoming open to the energy of creation to transform our consciousness from petty local concerns to a deeper, wider, and more pervasive awareness. Once we are made aware of this journey to wholeness, we cannot easily turn aside without losing our path. Part of this mysterious and wonderful life we have within us now is the potential to manifest the divine life on earth. The Spirit of Evolution is not far removed from us.

Many spiritual traditions within the East and West suggest that we are the hands and feet of the Jesus, the Buddha, the Allah, the Great Spirit. This teaching means that we hold enormous potential in our bodies, hearts, and minds to manifest divine life in our everyday world. These great teachers shared a common message - that spiritual awakening is an essential part of being human. Once we know this, we must in some way respond to this gift and responsibility. Even if that response is denial and turning away from this truth, we will then face the consequences of that choice and learn from that as well. All experiences are forms of learning.

This does not mean that people always grow from the learning. To grow demands that we actually listen and attend to the learning process and change our approach accordingly. Often, we must let go of old beliefs and habits of thought. At many turns we are required to let go of attachments before we can move on to a higher plane of existence. The spiritual manifest life does not come for free and is not an easy journey. Yet this pathwork is such an essential part of being human that we cannot deny the pull of our spirit. The hidden energy of the cosmos will listen to our choices and respond in kind.

On the brighter side, this book describes what may be called a sustainable approach to human development, nurturing spiritual insight, and wisdom, while harnessing energy for the wellbeing and balance of the worlds. The key is realising that we are a manifestation of the Great Spirit, and that we will be given the skills necessary to face the challenges ahead when we need them. While sounding simple, the profound implications of this realisation cannot be underestimated.

Our identity as human beings is built on three foundations.

Ecology: We are interconnected within the environment and the earth. Our existence depends in a symbiotic relationship with all that exists in nature.

Psychology: We are a manifestation of the consciousness of creation, and nature grows in awareness through our minds and hearts. Our relationships are guided by emotions, thoughts, and memories that inform not only how we live with family and what life choices we make, but that also direct the unfolding of our future and that influences the evolution of our species.

Spirituality: We are creative, gifted, and intuitive creatures who by nature seek meaning and purpose in our lives. As spiritual beings we need a roadmap back to becoming who we already are. Spiritual medicine is most powerful because by its nature it embraces and surpasses the other two. Another way to say the same thing is that body, mind, and spirit are the legs that hold up our existence. By getting to know how we work as human beings we can better form an internal road map of reality.

Once we have this, we can go as far as we wish in the realms of spiritual power.

This approach to personal development is about manifesting our strengths and amplifying them. We all have strengths and weaknesses. Focusing on the problems in life does not solve anything. By building on our strengths we compensate for our weaknesses and move beyond them. While growing in certain areas of life, the other places where we lack strength also tend to grow without our conscious awareness. This itself is part of the interconnected nature of our being. One day we wake up and realise how far we have come, and suddenly we can do much more than we could in the past. This approach to life needs to be simple, direct and honest. Yet simplicity also suggests depth and elegance. In this sense, the thresholds we face lead to deeper awareness of our world, our ecology. This expands our mental perception and our mind grows to embrace a heart-focused attention. From these emerge spiritual insight that is transformative and life changing. We grow through our strengths when we are interconnected with the world around us.

Methods of Self Awareness

The first step involved in this approach is just growing and building on our strengths. Along the way we learn to become more self-aware of who we are, and how we relate, with others and the environment. Most spiritual and cultural traditions place great merit on methods of self-awareness. Some call this examination of conscience, others self-analysis, some meditation, and others a process of critical self-awareness. Many approaches teach to do this kind of work every day, at least once, and often during the evening before going to sleep. At that time, we can remember the day and how we interacted with the world and people around us. We can ask ourselves how did things go? What worked? What needs more work in future? How did I respond? And from these questions arises deeper self-awareness, and from this comes an ability to let go of unnecessary baggage, and to learn from our mistakes.

Spiritual growth typically begins with self-awareness through confronting these kinds of personal blind spots. In the moment during the day we might not realise how we could act better, but by reflecting on our actions we can see different perspectives. What was a blind spot during an encounter can become a window of new perception later on.

The spiritual principles here are clear. All great teachers shared them. For instance, Jesus could not succeed in ministry without first facing his demons in the desert. The Buddha could not attain enlightenment without first facing the shadow of human suffering. Christians teach the notion of repentance leading to salvation. Alcoholics Anonymous teach that admitting powerlessness is the first step before reaching out to a Higher Power for assistance. In counselling psychotherapy, we say that the first step is accepting that you need help while reaching out for that help, and this means that your heart and mind are open to change.

At this time in our collective history human beings have become isolated from sources of help. We set ourselves apart from other people and from the Creator and from Life. We also prevent ourselves from finding the keys inside that create a better life. The conveniences of the modern day have ironically helped toward increasing this isolation and have made us less flexible and less open to change. We more or less expect life to give us a good deal and we have high expectations about our standard of living, but we are emotionally and spiritually poor. Part of this isolation we can observe is that we are lacking an ability to connect with our environment. We fail to understand how to co-exist with nature and the other creatures that inhabit this planet. We no longer know how to live with ourselves, and so fill up space with music, television, travel, entertainment, and a fast-paced lifestyle. But the reality is that people are not made to sustain these kinds of isolation-based and addictive behaviours.

Human beings are meant to have a balance between periods of work, times of play, moments of silence, and allowing the body-mind-spirit to rest and revive. In western cultures we have no contemporary meaning for fallow-time; that space where we can just be and abide with the day. In most other cultures there is a sense of the quality of life relating to just being alive and enjoying the moment, rather than always doing something to fill the gap. Finding this way of being is important to maintaining health and wellness.

This attentiveness to the moment can easily help us in so many ways, because we know that there are larger ecological forces impacting our daily lives. No longer are people immune from the wider challenges to our economy, where global events have made the social world around us more pliable and impacting on our personal survival. In the same way, we can no longer assume that our own struggles can be divorced from larger ecological, social, and economic issues.

Identity Crisis and Healing

Both levels of crisis, the personal and the ecological, indicate fundamental problems in the personal, social, and planetary spheres. We carry this energy around in us every day, an energy, often subtle and unconscious, of being out of balance. Those who are spiritually in-tune comment that they are aware of how much the shifts in human planetary imbalances actually impacts on their daily lives, their sense of personal health, and their state of mind.

Healing the divisions between self, society, and the ecological systems of the earth is a grand task. Ironic that this change is dependent on a fundamental and simple shift in human awareness and identity. For most of us who live in a built society, I believe this change requires something akin to a spiritual crisis of identity. All indications suggest that a large number of people are experiencing just such a crisis at personal and social levels. Many of us take on this crisis as an inheritance from our parents and grandparents.

We can be clear in our thinking, transparent and honest. This crisis is something we need to approach with a level head. It is not about blame. We need to become part of the solution. As the old saying goes, if you are not part of the solution, you are part of the problem. Even while our circumstances have been largely created by the choices of our forefathers and foremothers and then continued and escalated in recent times by our choices, we need to go beyond this kind of defeatist thinking. There are ways forward. Rather than exempt us individually from the responsibility of owning these poor choices, we need to take personal responsibility even if we have not personally caused the situation. This takes a lot of guts. Each of us participates in our collective history. Our future depends on each person's choice.

The micro psychological mirrors the macro ecological. In many ways we see these overlap in significance. Unless we can agree on a global ethic of responsibility and care for our environment, the human species will face increasing threat of extinction. But this same teaching applies to our psychology. Care for the body is the beginning of care for the environment, and vice versa. The future of humanity lies within our hands. Each and every human being on this planet plays an important role in our collective evolution. We each can take on some responsibility for our own healing and for finding a lasting peace and the restoration of ecological balance. Personal growth and planetary healing are one and the same story. It was only after realising a basic shift in identity that we were able to make many changes in lifestyle and thus bring the self into balance. Personal transformation has great ripple effects.

Over the years our life touched others. They moved on to influence other people beyond our immediate sphere. The second generation of people who did not know us personally went on to share with others. This third generation continued to pass on knowledge and insights. Before you know it, you have literally touched thousands of people. This is especially true when you offer things to people with the clearly communicated intention that they one day pass on what you are offering, so that the goodness will continue. I like to think that we become skilled in spreading the infection of kindness, which for me expresses the sum total of all knowledge and wisdom that can be made available and is practical in daily life.

As many people understand all too well, even changing our eating habits can be an enormous and often impossible goal unless there is a fundamental inner change within the person that motivates the external behavioural change. At the global level the same challenges are facing human communities around the world. Our identity must change before we will be able to address the great concerns of hunger, poverty, and war in a way that will sustain lasting and enduring systems of justice. We are at war in our bodies when we fight against our innate spiritual identity. Who we were created to be already exists inside of us. If we fall away from our personal path in life, we face the consequences. So, the global and the personal are one and the same, and both create waves of energy that expand outward.

A great cleansing needs to occur in our bodies, our communities, and in our societies. Spirits of greed, envy, selfishness and control hang heavily over many of our lives. Multiple layers of hurt and trauma have become such a regular part of our lives that we are normally unable to see how deeply confused and lost we have become. Only a crisis of great importance appears to cut through the fog of our minds and allows us to see the larger picture.

Habits of Thought

As we stand on a shadowy threshold of incredible dangers that threaten to destroy our ability to live healthy lives on this planet, each person with a conscience must ask important questions about what, in fact, it means to be human. To be human means that we are spiritual beings created to give of ourselves more than we take. But to live this truth is another matter entirely. To be human means that we would sacrifice our lives for others and for the planet – but to act on this altruistic belief requires courage.

The Native path teaches that we will take only what we need for today to survive. When we take, such as when we eat the fruit of the earth or when we eat the flesh of an animal, to stay healthy we need to pray and be aware of the life energy and gift of that being that gave its life so that we may live. In a sense we commune with the spirit of the animal and it becomes part of us. This process of communication between creatures only remains sustainable and balanced when we are spiritually aware and when we are prepared to give back something of ourselves. In this way we begin to understand where we sit within the greater scheme of life. This takes humility.

At the core of our being there needs to be a deep abiding respect for every living thing. When this respect is lost human behaviour falls out of balance and human systems become twisted out of proportion. We can see this happening in so many areas. For instance, when sea fish are kept in small containers to grow until they are ready to go to market. They are swimming in such small areas and in great numbers that they may swim in their own waste and are fed by artificial means that promote optimal growth. The end result is dishonouring to the spirit, energy, and integrity of the creature that is mistreated for human selfish gain. Fish were not created to live in a plastic cage. We reap what we sow, as less healthy fish do not nourish the human body.

Where respect is not paid adequately, lesser respect comes back. The nature of reality is karmic and remains as such to maintain balance. When the karmic debts are not paid, less and less benefits will exist to sustain and ongoing prosperous life.

This also is a form of identity crisis. We may not even be aware of these principles nor of the ways we could correct our path and way in life. For the most part, the western system and habit of thought has edited out so many points of ancient wisdom precisely so that the corporate colonial powers could maintain hegemony.

In our doctoral work we traced these systems of thought in relation to homophobia as a western cultural construct from the medieval period through to present day psychotherapy. This is only one example of the systems that human beings can generate. Like in personal growth over the years, individuals also come to terms with habits of thought and values that become counterproductive and that backfire later in life. We may have taken on a belief early in life based on a negative experience. Years later that belief no longer works; and we find ourselves in a marriage or adult partnership where the underlying beliefs and values creates problems and no longer functions. We find we are in continual cycles of conflicts that we do not understand. It can take a great deal of personal as well as cultural insight to examine issues of which we are not normally conscious.

Courage, humility, and respect are essential qualities of existence that arise from the fabric of reality. They are part of what we call the 'original teachings.' This is another way of saying that within creation itself we can observe, listen, and learn ways of living that arise from the universal laws of nature. These laws and the lore or stories that grow up around them are the heart and spirit of indigenous wisdom teachings. These laws are built into the energy, ebb, and flow of every moment of every day and can be observed in all creatures great and small. The old law exists in rock, hill, tree, and all manner of creatures that inhabit the Sacred Worlds of our Ancestors.

Reconnecting

Our cosmos is neither static nor void of mystery. Our Earth World is only one of the many Sacred Worlds that interact and influence our existence. While getting to know the self and empowering the self to grow, we also need to re-connect with the worlds around us. The World Beneath the Earth is another realm of existence that interacts and influences our lives. We would be better off if we paid more respect to the ground and the deep layers of Mother Earth beneath us. Instead we allow enormous mining and extraction of chemicals from the deep earth, and we stand by when methods of violence are enacted that fracture the earth's crust. We will pay the price for these actions and lack of actions. This is not the place to explore all the Sacred Worlds of our cosmos, so suffice it to say that there is much involved with inspiring self-awareness and growth in spiritual power.

Intimate to this growth is coming to terms with the challenges of society and making personal decisions to resist the status quo. For example, we are seeing more and more clearly that mass production cannot always maintain balanced and sustainable practices that are in tune with the wisdom inherent in the ecosystem. Beef and poultry production are obvious examples of mass systems that have become out of balance because of unsustainable artificial practices. The threats to human health caused by these approaches cannot be underestimated, nor can these problems be isolated and sanitised. Problems spill out into surrounding ecosystems and influence the whole food chain. The ripple effects continue onward.

It is important to realise that these examples are not isolated. Beneath the values of the modern world is a fundamental disregard for respecting human life and the natural order of things. This approach to life may have begun with the colonial expansion of Christianity as a state religion many hundreds of years ago, and then spread by the growth and power of the Catholic Church during the middle ages.

Likewise, the industrial revolution over the past three to four hundred years has increased the pace and power of human intervention in the environment. From having spiritual dominion over the earth that once meant that we were responsible as stewards and custodians, we have become heartless overlords of a perceived lifeless rock we call the planet earth. This perception and its selfish gain could not be further from the truth. In this attitude of contempt for creation, we see a widespread crisis of meaning across all western countries that has spread around the world.

People need to change. Social systems must also change so that the fundamental philosophy that guides our decisions is based in a global ethic of care for the future of our children and our beloved planet. A universal spirit of giving more than we receive needs to become the driving force behind economic decisions and political power. Actions at all social and political levels need to be based in a spirit of responsibility that brings us back to basic spiritual values of protecting and nurturing our relationship with local ecosystems.

Joseph Randolph Bowers

No One is an Island

It is with these thoughts that I consider the arts and sciences of personal transformation. Indeed no one is an island. Our most intimate lives are connected within a wider ecology. The awakening arising now in humanity reconnects us with our true identity.

In this context, we rely on several strands of knowledge. Western spirituality and mysticism provide enormous insight. Counselling psychotherapy gives us many practical tools and a way to build resourceful values and beliefs. Personal development as a field of practice opens pathways to growth and potential. Honouring indigenous traditions provides grounding in ecological and balanced values and approaches to all of the above.

By taking up the path of personal transformation we can open our hearts and minds to a new change that can sustain a rewarding and spiritually powerful life. Modern therapeutic approaches are one of the more popular pathways to engage in personal development.

Yet these modern methods echo ancient and long-standing indigenous cultural traditions. From these thresholds of self-therapy and mutual encouragement, we have the stepping-stones laid out before us that lead back to the Sacred Grove where we can once again raise the Cup of Blessing. We can find our way home. These methods manifest hidden spiritual thresholds of human potential, while activating our creative power and insight.

How to Read this Book

A brief word on how to read this book. The text is designed for personal reflection and study. Each chapter ends with activities in sync with recording your ideas, thoughts, feelings, and awakenings in a personal journal.

The idea of the 'journal' is explored as we go along, and can be any form of recording, expressing, and manifesting your journey. Some people are drawn to written journals, others to mediums of art like painting or drawing. Whatever suits you; find a means to express your learning journey.

Several reviewers mentioned the book is very suitable to small group discussion. Engaging a small group of friends or taking this book into an existing book-reading club are both tremendous ideas. You will benefit by hearing the questions, responses, and life-stories of other people.

Learning with others is often the best possible way to engage in personal and transformative work. Other readers suggested a church reading circle, a local library group, or an online forum. We can imagine that an emphasis on journaling might inspire many people to blog reflections after reading the chapters.

With personal transformative work in mind, the book is written for self-development but also as a guide while travelling through counselling. For this reason, many therapists and other professionals will enjoy reading this book for personal growth as well as to assess its utility for clients.

Clients may suggest working through the book while seeing a counsellor. Psychotherapists may recommend the book to clients during therapy as a companion volume to facilitate reflections. The book has also been used after a course of four to six sessions of therapy; suggested as a follow-up to reinforce the themes of personal transformation and empowerment arising during the therapeutic process. We are told by several therapists that they gave a copy to clients for this reason. Their doing this coincides with therapy outcome studies that reinforce the notion that a letter or resource that is given by a therapist to a client is often taken quite seriously and tends to be given at a time when a person is most receptive and impressionable. The positive aspects of this situation suggest that offering a book of this kind to a client who is ready for this can go a long way to helping them learn the skills, capacities, and kinds of awareness that they need.

As a guide and companion during psychotherapy the book is paced over eight sessions. For optimum practicality, the time between sessions needs to account for the reading capacity and time needed to adequately reflect, do activities, and engage in journal writing in preparation for the next session. Some people might take two weeks, others three or four weeks between sessions.

For this reason, working through this book within a therapy program can be paced over two to six months depending on the circumstances. It might be useful to have sessions in between chapters to offer additional time for assimilating and integrating the many themes of personal development into your own identity and sense of self.

Counselling psychotherapists and psychologists will benefit by using this book for self-care, personal growth, and professional development. Therapists in training will benefit greatly by engaging the experiential learning processes, discussing their experiences in groups, and having their instructor guide them through the integrative methods involved.

Therapists in supervision will get much from gaining deeper self-awareness through the activities. Discussing these with a clinical supervisor could provide a holistic pathway to integrating experiential knowledge with therapeutic skills in practice.

Likewise, we have used this material as the basis for spiritual retreats. Over a four-day weekend, we have engaged the activities and certain reflections within a concentrated and focused way. Although we tend to tailor the materials to the people involved, many of the same content is used. So as not to distract the participants from experiential awareness in the moment, we never tend to give the book to retreatants before or during the retreat. However, we do give them a copy of the book at the end of the retreat during a session that may incorporate a form of 'graduation ceremony' to acknowledge and pay respect to the work that they have done and will continue to do as the days and weeks unfold.

A more advanced series of retreat experiences may then utilise our other book, 'Solitude Awakens: The Heart, Forest, Mountain Way.' As a more detailed and reflective process, we tend to engage online study and/or reading of this book before, during, and after retreat experiences.

This being said, we have found the materials in both books incredibly useful to adapt to a course or program in spirituality and personal growth.

The first activity that follows below is in the form of a spiritual agreement. The values suggested providing an optimum inner environment for personal transformation and spiritual awakening.

It only makes sense to plant a seed in rich soil and then to tend and water the seed. This book is like the watering jug to assist in your pathwork. You are the one who will make this journey worthwhile. When you are ready to sign the agreement, you are also ready to step on the threshold to living a more fulfilling life.

Stardust Awakens

My Spiritual Agreement

I _____

Print Full Name

Agree to open myself to new insight.

To allow myself to grow spiritually.

To awaken the spirit within.

I understand and appreciate that,

- This process may be challenging at times.

- All good things worth doing in life often take effort and persistence.

- Patience is part of my learning, while having compassion for my needs and those of others.

Joseph Randolph Bowers

I _____

    Name

Further agree to,

Listen to Life around me,

Attend to new meanings that may arise in my waking and dreaming,

Try on a humble heart and mind,

Be a little more willing to admit my weaknesses,

Be a bit more open to acknowledge my strengths,

Respect myself a tad bit more in mind and body,

Listen to my inner voice,

Pay heed to my feelings, intuitions, and insights,

Pay attention to how life changes during this learning process, and

Practice one spontaneous act of kindness each day whether to myself or ideally with another.

Stardust Awakens

I _____
        Name

Also agree to,

Take things one step at a time,

Learn to release fears and anxieties in positive ways,

Breathe. Slowly and deeply. One breath at a time.

Honour the Power and Wisdom of my family's heritage and traditions.

Give goodness and loving kindness to my work, projects, children, and to their children to come.

Allow the Mystery of Life to be a source of strength,

Keep an open mind.

Signed, _____
        Your Signature

On this _____ Day of _____ In the Year _____
        Number   Month   Number

Joseph Randolph Bowers

1 Ground: Between the Worlds

Upon the ground we feel, we stand

Into Her heart we fear to go…

Earth rattles beneath us, quaking

Calling, Beckoning;

To find our self, embracing.

Coming from rural Nova Scotia, Canada, the land and the sea along with the culture of my upbringing had great influence in life. When we were growing up, we were not taught who or where we came from. For many reasons our heritage was not discussed. In the early days, we just lived and got on with life. What was most important for a young boy in those times were siblings, parents, extended family, neighbours, and of course, the open forest, lakes, and bog lands behind our home. My best friend during those childhood times was a German Shepard who early on had carried me on his back like a horse, and who walked with me through the forest. The magic of those years still provides rich inspiration. As childhood turned into young adult life, the solitary orientation within led on one hand to reaching out to others with a healing heart, and on the other hand to increasing discomfort with the conflicts and harsh energy of social life.

Some formative memories are around realising a sense that other kids noticed something different about us during the school years. We lived a 'mainstream' life for the most part, just another family trying to make a go in the rising middle class of the 1960s and 70s. What I didn't know back then and only came to realise as an adult was that my father came from a working-class family of mixed racial origins that held many of the secrets of our identity. But cultural identity back then was not defined by race so much as by the melting-pot mentality of middle-class Canadian consumer culture. To really understand many of these experiences requires an adult point of view that is informed by history, social awareness, and political wisdom.

Therefore, it is easy to say that the process of understanding being different took the better part of twenty-five years. And quite unusual for most peers, life led us to take up a lifetime of study, research, scholarship, teaching and professional practice, oriented towards solving some of the riddles left by the silence of those early years. What began as a quest to explore the forests and lakes led to a spiritual search for reconnecting with the deep past and with the undercurrents of identity that later in life came to define what is most important in life. These words are chosen wisely as they express the heart and spirit of the message in this book. Coming to terms with our true identity is of primary importance if we wish to find peace and to move on with life in an authentic and meaningful way, without any hidden ghosts or skeletons in the closet.

Eventually, many years later, work led to digging up the evidence of several layers of family's heritage. Study and research uncovered a long winding story that led back to 1652, with the immigration of one Michel Richard into what was called Acadia, a now extinct French colony in the respected national boundaries of Mi'kma'ki, the land of the Mi'kmaq First Nation. During those early years of settlement, relations between the Mi'kmaq and the French were respectful, signified by the King of France granting citizenship to the Mi'kmaq people. A different attitude existed then of mutual regard, cultural exchange, sharing of language, resources, ceremony, and family life. This was why it was a natural course of events for a French Acadian ancestor to marry into the Mi'kmaq nation.

From 1652, to the present day, a rather long story unfolds, and a fascinating and extremely sad story. The demise of the French colonies under what was to become a British stronghold factors centre stage. Symbolised by the building of the Citadel Hill in Fortress Halifax, built not so much for the purposes of war with France, but for a powerful message to the Mi'kmaq Nation that mutual respect was nothing to do with how the British would proceed in their colonial efforts.

Thus, while living and working in Australia, we travelled home to Nova Scotia in eastern Canada, and reconnected with Mi'kmaq First Nation and French Acadian heritage and culture. By this time, my father had passed over several years prior. Before he passed, he shared stories of our origins.

These things were never discussed when we were kids. Part of the reason was that the politics of race had been associated with conflict, war, and poverty for too long and for too many generations. It had become embedded in our unconscious memory to stay silent, not rock the boat, and to never cause waves by discussing politics, religion, culture, or racial issues. Only after extensive research did this macro-social psychology make sense to me. Human beings internalise transgenerational unresolved issues that are passed down to us by our parents, grandparents, great-grandparents, and beyond. These inherited patterns are now a commonly accepted and central layer of social theory as well as the therapeutic theory and practice.

Imagine how much it meant to realise that early childhood connections with the land, lakes, and sea of youth held layers of historical meaning. Imagine growing up not knowing who your people are, while searching for them; and while feeling so empty inside. Imagine having visions all during your childhood and young adult life that are associated with the trees, moss, crawling creatures, winged, and four legged creatures, and the finned creatures in the deep waters – never knowing why. Never realising that your innate sense of kinship among creation was part of your genetic heritage.

Imagine never being able to share these visions with others in your family or at school, knowing they might look at you like you are mad; like they don't want to know you anymore. Imagine picking up on feelings from other people and not knowing what to do with them, and later realising that you could in ways read people's hearts but no one in your world shared that ability. No one could even recognise or understand what you were going through. All these elements later made sense because they fit perfectly within the cultural beliefs and possibilities that are openly acknowledged by Mi'kmaq extended family who later in life welcomed us back into their midst.

These early experiences of being an empath, seer, and mystic were clouded in a lack of understanding. This we believe led to a long-lasting sadness during youth. When looking back there was nothing in the boy himself to create such a deep sense of aloneness and darkness. In many children and youth, we see forms of acting out as well as 'acting in' where kids isolate and protect themselves through various means.

Internally there was a search for some form of light and hope. In our world then, there were many energies; parents focused on making a go and building a home; sisters looking to dating and growing into adults; peers seeking drugs and alcohol for a quick sensory high and to drown out the pressures they were facing all around them; church members looking to influence others for their own ends; and teachers in school bent on surviving until retirement. In many ways the challenge was also the greatest blessing. Life enforced solitude. We were left alone to our own devises to sort out the conflicting energies of the world. This pressing need led to observing and learning more about people and to attending to inner psychic realities.

For many reasons, during young adult life we turned to mystical experiences and to a great deal of time alone in the forest. Mother Nature was safe and trustworthy even while commanding respect. Instinctively, a spiritual orientation opened up and kept us safe from the drugs and alcohol that dominated the lives of peers. School was a violent place. Except for a miracle, we would have quit school and never gone to university.

One solace during those dark times was the gift of music. At first, we explored playing drums and percussion in a concert band. Later we found that playing guitar expressed hidden emotions. Surprise, surprise, we discovered a singing voice; and even more astonishing that people loved and enjoyed our signing.

We quickly realised major leaps forward in composing spiritual folk music. This led to taking over the planning of liturgy and ceremony in the local church, as well as conducting youth and adult choirs. These years of working with music and planning liturgy were formative experiences. The study of music and liturgy introduced us to the western Christian mystical tradition. Then later, during a bachelor degree in religious studies and philosophy we consolidated this study by further explorations in medieval and Franciscan mysticism, as well as eremitic and monastic contemplative spirituality.

The main emphasis of the western earth based spiritual traditions surrounds a reverence and respect for the closeness of the divine energy. Earth-based spirituality places God and Goddess within our bodies and in nature around us. Creator is not far away. The Great Spirit is close to us and in our skin-time. These undercurrents can be found in the Christian gospels, particularly when you read them in light of ancient Hebrew mysticism while filtering out the Pauline institutionalism of the corporate church that followed the time of the gospel narratives of the life of Christ.

So much of Christian mysticism comes alive in the pre-Pauline vision of gospel simplicity; and in many respects these intuitive and astute resonances have been confirmed through the discoveries of the Dead Sea Scrolls and other gnostic scriptures that were circulating during the first centuries but that were subject to censorship by the emerging colonialism that built on the Pauline fixations with incorporation and law making. Conspiracy theories of those early centuries say that the imperial guard and select families constructed the canonical gospels and selected Paul's letters for inclusion in the accepted doctrines, precisely to adopt a colonial ethos that would support a centralised empire. From this view, it is not surprising that during the second to fifth centuries that the desert fathers and mothers left the cities and churches to protest among the first generations of the earliest of reformations. From our present day, during a post-gnostic gospel and post-dead-sea-scroll discovery perspective, many of the early movements, currents, and changes tend to make more sense; particularly as the early centuries. Also, the accounts of the life of Christ leave so much unsaid, and seemingly strategically so; and with an outcome where silence and hiddenness increases the mechanisms of power.

In the Native tradition, by contrast, within transparency we find Divine Life through human experience, and through kinship with the land and sea around us. This innate divinity and immanence of Life as Sacred is expressed, in one sense, through the humanity and incarnation of Jesus. In a pre-Pauline gospel universe Jesus of Nazareth is a brother and compatriot; not so much, if at all, a Lord and Master. Not only so, but Jesus is both brother and sister, mother and father, feminine and masculine, and most deeply and mystically a Two Spirit being – a being of light and mystery. A fully embodied expression of loving kindness. This Jesus is a Medicine Keeper who gives away all that she and he holds dear. For this being of light holds nothing and gives freely with open arms and hands. As a brother, sister, mother and father, Jesus is part of the intimacy of family. In this vision of Christ, we see Mother and Father, Goddess and God, as one being of light without division and without the structures of a monolithic political system of canon law, doctrine, and profane theology that supports divisions, abuse, and power.

These values lead people to exploring other western earth-based cultural and spiritual traditions including the Pagan rural traditions across Europe; the Teutonic traditions of middle Europe and the Germanic tribes; the ancient and well documented Goddess and Matriarchal traditions that predated patriarchy and Christian history in France; and the deep Celtic mysticism of many tribes including old-Irish mythology that informs our bloodlines through our mother's side of the family. These led to undertake in-depth study of the Druid path among the British Druid Order, who offer a contemporary expression of the study and practice of earth-based spirituality and mysticism.

These studies and the fascination with culture and spirituality helped us to conclude that there are so many amazing benefits from understanding and honouring western mysticism as a unified body of knowledge, practice, and wisdom. Unfortunately, not many people have come to this conclusion. But there are those who are seeking.

By expressing openness to all of these paths people who tend toward an exclusive commitment to only one path do not abide well with the diversity of knowledge that we offer. Indeed, this approach is to recommend becoming grounded in one tradition before exploring others. Bloom where you are planted is the best and most simple way to say this.

Overall, it seems quite true today that most people start their spiritual journey by mixing and matching from many traditions, often without knowing what practice or idea comes from where. There is nothing inherently wrong with this approach. We all make do with what we have, what we know, and with our perspectives in each moment.

Across these years one thing led to another, and we regret nothing of the exploring. At every turn new insight and a deeper honesty and integrity grew within. The path was about listening internally for the signs and symbols of the Creator's mind. Seeking the signs of the times and discerning the movement of the Great and Holy Spirit for life and meaning each day. This way of life kept us on the edge of our seat, always anticipating the joy and childlike pleasure of learning. And during darker times, from unknown pathways and in even deeper uncertainly and shadows; eventually came glimmers of hope quite unexpected and dearly needed. This book expresses a small glimpse of the gems that we have learned along the way that might make your searching that little bit easier.

In these ways, it has taken many years to grow and understand identity within the context of these times. Only now as we grow older does the freedom to speak arise. Before this time, it seemed taboo in our culture and world to speak what was in the spirit.

As one of those youth who carried the burden of our collective Ancestor's unresolved conflicts, we became a bridge between many worlds. As a very reluctant healer and teacher and in spite of myself, it appeared that Great Spirit called us through visions and through many experiences. These have taught a great deal of humility and given deep abiding values. From this place of accepting human frailty it is very difficult to then be asked to teach what we know of the spiritual path.

In being an intensely spiritual youth, and a very private adult given to solitary life, we also stood outside of the culture of our peers. They were more interested in alcohol and drugs, partying, and sex. While we faced loneliness on a daily basis throughout youth, life also presented us with many insights into the underlying motivations and issues of our peers. The spirit and mind became attuned to the emotional frequencies of people. It was during these years that we began the path of becoming a healer.

Other strong influences on in development included Roman Catholicism and exposure to the Christian mysticism of the monastic traditions of the west. During formative years of working in the church, we were honoured to learn ancient practices of meditation and prayer from several elders. These practices gave a foundation for life by opening and nurturing a peace-filled disposition. Over the years we became familiar with many euphoric and charismatic altered states of awareness that seemed to blur the lines between this reality and the next. During youth and young adult years, spiritual visions came regularly and opened many pathways of perception. Many experiences of healing and helping people through words, deeds, healing-touch, and music were commonplace.

The first university degree in religious studies and philosophy was like a bridge into the wider western world of history, culture, and ways of thinking. As a young adult the theories we learned in university encouraged us to impose frameworks around spiritual experience. The rational world dominated life well into the 30s.

Like Peter Pan, we were forced to put 'childish things' behind as we are 'supposed to do.' By repressing an innate spiritual affinity; life changed dramatically. By putting aside and no longer trusting intuitive insight the years that followed were extremely painful and disconcerting. By denying ability in healing, the body became more and more blocked and sick.

At the time, we simply trusted the theories and perspectives of the intellectual world because there were no useful frameworks to understand our experience. In being different and having insights that don't fit today's world, wherever we turned we faced closed doors head on.

After nearly destroying life during a very dark period when suicide seemed like a viable option, in our youth we returned home and sought the help of a senior counsellor. He quickly took us under his wing and became a mentor and guide whose skill in reframing life allowed the awakening of a new path. He provided hope that had been lost. Redge Craig was his name. His example inspired us to become a counselling psychotherapist. With his support, we made major changes in order to undertake master degrees in ecological family therapy and then Rogerian person-centred counselling psychotherapy. These efforts offered another perspective from which to view human life and meaning. Indeed, it was counselling psychotherapy that helped to unpack the early years and to realise that life was not as bad as many people seemed to want us to believe. The greatest conspiracy is how people's innate goodness is concealed by habits of thought that see humanity as eternally flawed, sinful, and damned. Such a worldview is dark and foreboding and leads to hopelessness and despair. Indeed, through therapy we came to see how gifted we had been in past. How humanity is made of blessings. And how the more ancient and human cultural wisdom arises from cooperation and gifts of kindness. Once you see this longer view of history and culture, you realise how young and misguided Christianity has been over a very brief and momentary span of years.

It is true how the ugly duckling slowly transforms into a swan. At the same time, Peter Pan returns to his former glory and accepts his innate giftedness. He even discovers his love of men and opens his heart to being himself. But before all of that is even possible, Peter has to symbolically die to his false identity and be reborn as a spiritual being. Through that dark night of the soul, Peter needs to earn back his wings. He needs to become a Two Spirit being of light.

After gaining master degrees and while working in private practice, life took new turns when our father passed away. A dark night overshadowed life for some time. That itself is another story about facing the shadow of death, but a story best left for another time. Soon afterwards, a PhD scholarship led to study and teaching in Australia.

In symbolic and real terms, the years between youth and now have been about losing and regaining a core identity. Human development is like this. Ironically the most difficult part of life has been to accept a mystical and spiritual nature. Because of the western society we live in there was no place to freely explore spiritual experience in a way that honoured the western academic world because of the dichotomy that society, the culture of science, and the culture of religion all collectively place on spirituality versus intellectual life in today's world. This bipolarisation is responsible for untold suffering; even while this invisible cold war may artificially bolster each camp and their respective benefits to maintain a false sense of power, influence, control, and security of place.

Overall, coming to negotiate this socially unacknowledged but deeply embedded cold war of ideas was at the crux of many life-challenges. Once we found peace with the process of being a spiritual mystical being in a secular materialist world the other parts of life began to fall into place. As we advanced in degrees in the western academe, by making western material rationalism a new home; life became a living duality. This more than any other struggle causes enormous psychological anxiety for countless people today. In reconciling these issues, a deeper integration of being is realised. A wider understanding of western history and the developments of social psychology emerge in the heart-mind over time that shows you the depth of meaning and spiritual insight that are contained in our heritage. But to find this meaning we must go beyond what we are spoon fed in today's universities. Contemporary scholarship denies and overlooks the depths of wisdom found in western heritage precisely due to the extreme conflict of values that is being waged in the academe at this time. Not so much due to people actively engaged in an ideological cold war – because this struggle is transgenerational and people today do not realise, have not woken up, and the reality of the struggles will not come to light until the western psyche is ready to face the shadows.

These views make the current materialist-secular academe look terribly corporate and brittle. The values that govern the academe at this juncture of history, especially with the advent of technology and distance education methods, are values of commerce, economics, profit and gain. There is neither balance nor beauty in this culture. More than ever, the prestige of the academe has reached a peak and may potentially face decline precisely because of the hollow values that maintain academic status in society. Beyond the academe, as forms of social knowledge expand and as access to information continues to grow through technology, with any hope new forms of culture and science will emerge. The power of the academe to dish out knowledge may be challenged.

Walking between the worlds of spirituality, poetry and rational philosophy is, nay, a nearly impossible task. Being a bridge between cultures such as western mysticism and science is doomed to many failures of assumption, regardless how careful one tries to be. Manifesting an emerging ethic that is authentically integrative and holistic requires many challenges, upsets and false starts. Growing in wisdom does not occur through some blind acceptance of knowledge, nor does wisdom arise from merely observing beauty or spirituality. Wisdom grows only from hard work and learning from mistakes over many years, if not over many skin-times.

And here we will depart from the acceptable realms of rational materialist philosophy. In many ways experience contradicts the dogma of 'what we can see and touch, we can measure. And therefore, that is all that exists.' This materialism creates a grave misunderstanding of a more holistic empirical method. In traditional Aboriginal cultures such as in Mi'kmaq heritage, observation is at the heart of an Indigenous science. But this form of knowledge does not deny the existence of worlds and realities beyond what we can understand. Just as in western methods, where we use forms of induction and deduction, we come to terms with reality and make theory from our experience of observing and interpreting phenomena. But in the west, we are unique among all the cultures around the world because we are the only people presumptuous enough to not only assume but also to make it a dogmatic truth that all reality must be reduced to what we can measure in material forms. This core belief of the secular academe today does a grave injustice to the very nature of reality.

My approach celebrates and affirms the holistic and complex nature of the world as including many forms of knowing that do not easily fall to the limited methods of scientific observation held by the western academe. In this way we take a phenomenological approach – a big term that means simply that all manner of reality can be in some way experienced by people and needs to be respected as such. Rather than denying any form of reality, in this approach we keep an open mind, listen, observe and maintain plausibility.

Bernard Lonergan's work, in both theology and in the philosophy of insight, stands among some of the greatest contributions to modern scholarship. For a whole year we undertook a directed study reading Lonergan's great work 'Insight.' That tome led to understanding the complexity and elegant simplicity of the structures of human insight. From that study, over the years we have pondered various theories in light of the logic proposed in 'Insight' and have yet to see any theory come close to making as much sense.

Lonergan proposed that every human insight arises from our innate capacity to question. Our very nature is comprised of the ability and equipoise of questioning. We lean toward the next question as if our lives depended on asking, seeking and knocking for answers and further insights. This nature is integral to our every waking and sleeping moment. In our dreams the nature of reality opens up exponentially. Our potent-questioning-nature was part of the gift and curse that was given to us by Creator, and by our inability to keep anything sacred. We are driven by our questioning nature to turn over every rock and stone.

The Hebrew creation story suggests that the first created human beings entered the sacred garden set aside by the Creator for a special purpose. They were unable to stop themselves. Their inquiring minds would not rest until they ate from the Tree of Knowledge that contained the Seed of Life within the metaphorical apple. To gain that secret knowledge, gnosis, and to seek out the experience of insight, was perhaps the primary meaning of the metaphorical story. Humanity is consumed with an unwavering passion for knowledge as both a mystical experience and an intellectual knowing, which is what gnosis means in its more holistic sense. This quest for insight opens up new pathways. Whether this quality of humanity is part and parcel of the Original Intention or merely another mistaken happenstance of evolution, this dimension of our being came to define the nature of humanity.

Many similar indigenous stories from around the world suggest that human beings, whether soon after or long after the day of Creation, had to face their innate ability to choose between the energies and forces of life and death. To stand in that Circle of Creation and harness the power of divine energy comes down to simple acts – like eating an apple; feeding one's children; taking in a stranger; honouring a hospitality law, being kind, forgiving a wrong; and opening up knowledge to someone who asks even when you can see they will likely misuse that knowledge in future. And yet standing in the Centre of the Ceremonial Circle of Creation is more than a metaphor for being balanced and doing well in the world of men and women.

Learning the basic processes of Ceremonial Practice is part of the passageway toward coming to terms with greater spiritual knowledge, insight and wisdom. These Sacred Doorways lead to many hidden mansions within the 'Kingdom of God.' This is in some sense the Mass of Creation.

Back to the notions of western knowledge. Lonergan's basic proposal around the structure of human insight led us, later in life, to acknowledge the universal and yet culturally specific nature of inquiry. In the dominant western mind, research and inquiry are founded on a flatland view of knowledge. In some real way, the 'Roman' in the 'Catholic' needs to be renounced so that the 'catholic' as universal can ascend to clarity of insight. This epistemology initially results in very many rotten apples falling from the Tree of Life, resulting in environmental hardship, and causing the extinction of millions of species. By having based western knowledge in a separate value system from the age-old notions of the sacredness of all of life, the imperial, colonial, industrial and technological revolutions have known absolutely no boundaries in their destruction of ethical maturity.

Yet the very structure of human insight remains the same across this and other cultures. The primary difference is that value systems in other cultures do not exploit nature to such a degree. These other ways of believing in our essential relationship with the planet and her inhabitants create legal, ethical and moral foundations that assist people to respect Mother Nature in all her forms. Of course, no culture is without its shadows and dark times. But the point is that no culture on earth or over history has ever taken such a terribly exploitative disregard for Mother Nature as our present-day society.

Coupled with this is the way in which our western beliefs have been formed over the years and how we have come to relate to the dominant forms of contemporary western values. In many respects our generation's life's work is about offering critique of western approaches as quite inadequate to answer the deepest and most pressing questions facing humanity at this turn of history. Many of the pitfalls we have entered have consumed large sectors of society including the academe of the professions as well as the arts and sciences. Much of this critique is based in a wider appreciation for non-western methods, beliefs and values. All of these suggest alternative ways of honouring insight that arise within a more traditional human value system. These traditional frameworks are not the antithesis of science. Instead, they can give scientific inquiry and other forms of progress a moral centre upon which to grow in more balanced ways.

Lonergan suggested that human insight comprises the ability to choose one path over another. Innate within us is given a moral compass upon which to guide our actions. It was in this sense completely right for Adam and Eve to enter the sacred garden and to eat from the Tree of Life. To do so honoured the nature of their creation. To turn aside from this action would have also been a primarily sinful act. In this sense, original sin was to question and to act upon a question. And yet, because this is innate in our nature, to not question and not act would also be to sin. In the traditional Eucharistic feast of the early church the Act of Contrition included the phrase 'in what I have done and in what I have failed to do.' In a sense this deeper understanding of human nature is built into the fabric of western Christian mysticism. We are good to remember one essential mystery that is very often hidden and covered over by most every bishop of the imperial church. This mystery is that the word Eucharist means 'thanksgiving.' How could such a feast of thanksgiving given in loving kindness become not only an act of social control, but also of shame, fear, discrimination, and violence?

While we are betwixt and between are there certain lines that should not be crossed? The history of humanity suggests that boundaries will be violated. Even with this kind of philosophical acceptance of the human condition, the more mature understanding of experience in life suggests that a balance can be stuck once you have gone from one extreme to another and when you finally find your middle ground. This personal middle ground often comes at a very great price and after much exploration and marginalization. Over time you must accept that certain experiences will challenge the flatland view of western culture. Like any good social scientist you will have to let go of your preconceptions. You will have to accept a new view of reality.

At the same time, this discussion may help you to understand the importance of Indigenous forms of knowledge. Words like Creator, God, Goddess, Higher Power, and Great Spirit are metaphors for something that people experience in personal and intimate ways. Growing up within the woods, lakes and rivers of Eastern Canada we could never deny the power of nature nor put aside the presence of a Life Force experienced within simply observing and interacting with the environment. But this does not make a theist in the western sense of the term. Indeed, many people do not feel that First Nation spirituality is in fact a form of religion in the western sense. Instead, the native approach is a form of experiential awareness and personal awakening rather than an abstract theology. This direct personal process is meant to build relationships of honour and respect between people, and between people and entities in nature. Because of this background we have believed in the spiritual nature of the world as being interconnected and relational.

It is wholly plausible to remain an agnostic while believing in the divine nature of the world. And this complex way of knowing is based on what we know – not on what we believe is true. Beliefs have little to do with reality. Beliefs are like thoughts in the cognitive mind, they come and go like the clouds. In meditation practice, you learn to let go of thoughts and beliefs, even values. You come to terms with a deeper more experiential wisdom that is more expressed by the darkness of space between the planets than by the planetary bodies themselves. Afterall, the convergence of substance in the cosmos and in nature is simply that – a momentary collection of matter giving rise to actions of evolution and in some rare cases, life and consciousness. Enlightenment is a process of awakening to this reality all around and within; a far cry from the dogmatic-based salvation of ages past when people would kill each other because our saint was of a different colour of skin or clothing from your saint. But precisely, in our day, in these very generations now, humanity at least among the western children of Eve, there is an awakening that is emerging within the more pervasive spirit of evolution that may yet free the western mind from the dictates of past dogma.

Attending to a direct experience of life. We have in many relationships a finger pointing toward the plausibility of the existence of a Creator, God, Goddess, Higher Power or Spirit of Life, all metaphors for the evolutionary truth we dare not face.

As the truth may crush all our past beliefs. May open our being to freedom, to awakening, in the vast sea of the uncertain cosmos. No wonder the Buddha is such a radical figure for the western mind. We maintain that we will not know the Creator until we come face to face with the Higher Power at some time in future. Look in the mirror. And in this sense, we may remain an agnostic. Look at the flower blooming through the frost of winter. We observe and appreciate the spiritual qualities of life and evolution. Something more dawns.

It is also helpful to clarify that the words God or Goddess, Creator or Divine Being do not really mean some exterior objective Person who exists in this realm or another. The word 'God' does not mean an old man with white beard who sits on a throne in some heavenly realm. These words are projections, because all insight arises within. The word is a story, metaphor, a medicine. Do we use the word for more insight or to fool the mind and heart into some belief or idea?

The words are best used to speak of the Mystery of Life within all of us, no? These words are therapeutic! They can convey a much richer meaning that a poet, mystic, saint or crazy therapist can adequately express and understand. Divine nature is an integral part of the structure of our DNA, did you not realise yet? The so-called 'Divine' is woven into the fabric of atomic structures and exists as a part of the forces of movement, stasis, gravity, and the void of space. The power of the 'Divine' is seen in the notions of the Big Bang theory as much as within the very expansion of the universe. And this innate energetic life force we call Evolution, Creator, God or Goddess we can see in the forms of light and darkness, shadow and flame. Even in your childhood fears, and how you came to overcome your shadows of despair.

It seems very important in today's world to have a strong inner core of beliefs and values that actually make sense as well as provide a deep abiding inner strength and resilience when life throws us a curve ball. By taking the 'divine being' as a metaphor of other more important insights that we can actually experience, know and observe through subtler sensory stimulus the divine nature of reality is opened up all around us. Our emotional, intuitive and psychic abilities as human beings are actually well tuned to grasp a wider field of perception than are normally acknowledged.

In a similar manner we have come to accept that commonly held assumptions about life do not mean that these beliefs are true. For example, more recent western culture assumes that human beings are given only one life to live. In this belief we stand as a minority among the people of the planet. Contemporary beliefs no longer hold that an afterlife exists or even that our body's physical energy is transformed into something different. People today believe we just die, are cremated, become lifeless, and nothing remains. As a culture these beliefs show that we have come to the logical extreme of a materialistic philosophy. All of life is expendable.

When you basically grow up inside these beliefs, the culture you inhabit takes on values that grow from these beliefs. These too are projections – what will you project today? What world will you create?

If we turn into nothing when we die, we are also nothing when we live. We have no inherent relationship with the world around us. The absence of relational ethics gives rise to dehumanising cultural ways. The nature of underlying philosophies like these is that they determine the outcomes of what will follow – from beliefs arise values, ethics, morals and human actions. From these grow systems of law, governance, economy and education. From these come the ways in which we actually treat each other and the planet – so our beliefs actually do make an enormous difference. Contemporary materialistic empirical beliefs are so dangerous because they promote imbalanced ways of thinking, acting and forming social norms that tend to be heartless, cold, absolute, inflexible and unforgiving.

In the greater picture of things our beliefs can create the balance by which we can sustain our lives and the life of future generations. But these beliefs need to be well formed in the first place. Most people today never stop to consider their core beliefs, in part because they are like the background operating system of a computer. To see them we need to slow down, become self-aware, and ask questions about our ways of life, our values, our desires and our underlying intentions.

Effectively then, from a Lonergan type perspective on human insight, the parallel to empirical materialism is actually religious fundamentalism. In the same way, an expansionist imperial communist Marxism actually equates with a media driven capitalist materialism. All of these extremes deflate democratic freedoms that rest in a divine-human matrix of insight that is, at the base, completely and purely arising from evolutionary blessing and loving kindness. The key factor in common within every ideology is an absence of deep questioning of the self along with the renunciation of attachment within a process that seeks to gain a wider and more balanced perspective on reality. When we are grasped by this insight, we realise with empty hands that nearly every human belief comes from a process of how one insight leads to another… We also see how extremes of experience can lead to assumptions based in largely unconscious interpretations of reality. These may have historical significance. But they too are phantoms that must be renounced.

In other words, modern western philosophy did not evolve in a vacuum. One thing led to another. The extremes of western materialism arose from a historical reaction to other forms of extreme religious conflicts during the protestant reformation and continued to be deployed during the industrial revolution. The exploitation of nature throughout the industrial and technological age is justified in many ways by western humanism and materialism.

The origins of these modern philosophies were instrumental in the expansion of colonialism throughout the eighteenth and nineteenth centuries that provided the British Empire an assumptive right to dominate other cultures and lands. More recent events like World War II also had a huge influence on the formation of western materialism; just as much as religious fundamentalism in the west and east have contributed to the current theories of meaning that people espouse. Far eastern constructs from ancient imperial and Confucius thought, through to the contemporary communist Chinese party's ideology also express this yearning of humanity for primary insight that exists quite apart from social and collective systems that seek to dominate, control, influence, and self-replicate. The personal parallel to these wider social phenomena relate to how people form unbalanced beliefs based on largely emotional and fabricated projections that are in fact reactions to difficult or overly positive experiences. Beliefs formed during either trauma or moments of elation tend to result in overly simplistic linear structures in the neurological construction of beliefs.

Thus, the structure of balanced insight is one of the key ideas we need to grasp to understand well-formed beliefs. When all of society today tends towards extremes there are few people around who can adequately point in the right direction. This is why my statements do not rest in 'fact' so much as in an attitude of plausibility. The spiritual path rests on personal experience. We cannot provide the answers. But we can point you in the direction where you might find answers for yourself, while pointing out to you the inherent dangers along the way. Indeed, this basic attitude has grown mostly through encountering Aboriginal Elders whose way of looking at the world was both deeply reverential and profoundly open minded. The two can easily go together – something that we have overlooked in the west in recent centuries.

This is why we so easily know self as a mystic, shaman, healer and spiritual being. These definitions do not box you in but challenge you to remain humble and open to learning. They do this because they are not projections of roles but speak to processes of learning and growth in personal transformation. They do not fix the identity like a label. At the same time, it is true that you can know self as a scholar, social scientist and counselling psychotherapist. These are roles that we play in society. They too are illusions.

As a contemporary being we hold these apparent contradictions together as important elements in the way this era experiences the world. By contradictions we do not mean that the different views conflict or that one is right and the other is wrong. What we mean is that contradiction is really a paradox. A paradox is a phenomenon where both or many parts of the picture stand together in spite of what 'common sense' dictates ought to be opposite, conflicting, abnormal or dysfunctional. Much of life is a paradox rather than a clearly defined truth. This way of being is actually itself implied in the spiritual and cultural perspectives that have guided all of the world's best work.

But don't fool yourself. Living with paradox is not to take the easy road. By seeing things in this open-ended way, you need to abide with the ways this approach may contradict your beliefs while transforming your life. This state of paradox can create what we call cultural dissonance. If you have ever heard a guitar played that is out of tune and sounds harsh to your ears, you will know what dissonance means.

This kind of discomfort and unease seems at first to be abnormal and even dangerous. But paradox comes with an innate sense of 'this is right, even though it feels uncomfortable.' This is why most people do not get what paradox feels like. Most of contemporary life including the higher degrees of the academe is based in binary systems that allow for simple correlations. Little of modern life is about living with paradox. People today cannot abide with anything that feels uncomfortable. They want to fill that space with a pill, a drink or some noise. They want to live in simple binaries that just explain away all of life. But paradox exists in the more hidden spaces of silence, where we can ponder the meaning of life. Not an idle task. Those who go there on the part of humanity take the greatest risk and face demons that others avoid.

While living within the space of trans-cultural paradox, we may risk people from all cultures misunderstanding and misrepresenting our work. Again, it is much easier for people to think that other cultures are foreign and of no consequence. From these trains of thought come racism and prejudice. People tend to discount other points of view that seem different. But the cultural and spiritual path of enlightenment embraces and resolves the struggles of humanity. All forms of suffering eventually dissipate. All internalised un-resourceful beliefs including inherited patterns of thought that lead to suffering will eventually subside.

Children do not necessarily question the values they receive. Rather their very dependence on adults for survival promotes a kind of 'go with the flow' attitude in children. Young adults on the other hand can easily question most and everything handed down to them, and rightly so. In their psychology is built-in the structures of insight which arise in the higher cortical functions; largely linked to the evolution of the frontal lobes. These functions of the brain carry much of cognition and awareness of the complex nature of present reality as well as the bulk of short-term memory.

As we grow older the fires of youth tend to dwindle, and we come to accept much of what life throws at us. But we also become dull if we do not exercise the higher functions of our psyche and spirit that are innate to youth. At times, our bodies throw us into crisis because we have maintained unsustainable approaches to living and thinking. The longstanding notions of midlife crisis were one expression of this middle-class breakdown of identity so that something more integral and honest might emerge in later life.

The path of spiritual enlightenment is actually a way to kick-start and keeps the fires of youth burning throughout life. The positive side of this is that spiritual power grows in a person who dedicates their life to spiritual growth. The downside is that spiritual growth demands a degree of focus and commitment that tends to be rare in today's world. At the centre of the spiritual life rests basic attitudes like that of paradox that actually sustain an open mind-heart-spirit. These patterns of thought and attitudes of being promote a form of depth perception that some people only achieve much later in life, and for many, only at the hours prior to death.

However, don't you feel it would be much more meaningful to be completely awake now rather than waiting until you are on your deathbed? Or worse still, that you might never know that pure awareness of being because you never took the time or effort – and then something happened that ended your life prematurely such as a car accident or illness?

All is not lost, as we can come to these mystical states of being-awake at any time and with the right conditions. After taking this path since youth these many years have been most interesting. At times we have completely regretted the spiritual vows to serve humanity until we awaken as a collective. But these vows are a part of our spirit – vows taken over many lifetimes. These promises have bound us to the wheel of human suffering and re-learning the simplest lessons over and over again. But within or behind those spiritual vows is an evolving awareness. Some people might call this wisdom, ancient insight, or ancestral knowledge. But in an experience of observing people and the world, everyone and everything has these innate stores of power. Some of us learn how to access these data streams more readily than others. The 'old law' as it is called by many of my Aboriginal friends and family is not only part of us two legged creatures. We share this store of environmental and planetary memory with every element of nature and with all sentient and non-sentient beings that inhabit the cosmos.

Also important is to understand that none of us is only one static person but made up of many qualities, capacities and insights. We grow over time. We embrace different perspectives, learning, and values that are expressed in many cultural and spiritual manifestations. While growing older the path in life asks us to explore many cultural and spiritual traditions. These form a kind of synthesis.

In the centre of the circle is personal identity. Around that inner circle are linkages to different cultural traditions, each having its own integrity and importance. When taken together they form a complete picture of a person's value systems, beliefs, creative capacities and spiritual potentials. Most people's "synthesis" includes family history, culture, and perhaps other areas like religious background, school and learning, and social connections in today's world. As we grow and take on additional layers of meaning, exploring other cultural worldviews, we can expand our awareness and our identity is changed accordingly. Over time the pathwork asks you to renounce all of these things to let go into a higher state of being.

Others may not understand these things, and that is OK. In reality all people have this capacity for learning and growth in identity. For most people, the same dynamic is happening but is grounded in immediate family and cultural life. But we can all relate how complex and dynamic today's world actually has become – we are all a synthesis of many world cultures that in many ways enrich our lives, blending and complementing each other in our daily lives.

In a First Nations cultural view, identity is also very flexible. Even more so, a traditional cultural sense of self is fluid and can change shapes. Consciousness can shift from being within a human point of view to another animal's perspective. We can walk with our brothers and sisters among many "nations" including the Wolf Nation, the Eagle Nation, the Bear Nation and the Turtle Nation. Through experiences of vision and connection, we can move between worlds and learn many sacred and cultural lessons from among different species. Over our lifetime, in the Native Way, we may change our names when we come to identify with a new way of being. We can grow to such an extent that our spirits may no longer be merely "human" but may embrace a far wider spectrum of reality. The advanced degrees of identity development involve opening ourselves to new perspectives and learning.

In this world there are many relations to explore. Indeed, the path that we follow is one of balancing value systems while inherently siding with a numinous sense of the creative. Be this as it may, it is more important to hold up a vision of hope than to remain silent. So, we can release these illusions of conflict by accepting the complexity of life, acknowledging who we are and getting on with the work at hand. These core values of synthesis and integration may help to explain how we have come to balance the paths of Counsellor Psychotherapist, Educator, Social Scientist, Mi'kmaq Pipe Carrier and native Spiritual Healer. Likewise, taking these perspectives and applying them to create an approach to therapy and learning has enabled us to chart a course for personal and spiritual development from a unique perspective that is not terribly common in today's world. The approach is integrative, holistic and transpersonal but is also grounded in respect for culture, personal history, familial heritage, and learning capacities. Personal transformation is both an art and a science.

Anyone can relate to this process. For example, many clients over the years are focused on simply surviving daily life. They might want to get along better with a family member. They might want to move beyond patterns of behaviour that have them stuck in counterproductive relationships.

These practical wishes are great examples of how people seek a synthesis between inner values, their relational world, and their desire to grow. We are all more than what we feel. We are more than what we think. We are more than our problems that occupy our focus for today. We are indeed more than our limited beliefs about our self, and the spiritual worlds around us provide linkages with that "more" so that we can transform ourselves over time into spiritual human beings. We are given divine potential to manifest the powers of creation in our lives and in the world. From this ground of being we can journey further into realms that even angels fear to tread – into the heart and soul of humanity.

Activity 1 Personal Story

Each chapter of this book is dedicated to one 'Sacred Direction,' (East, West etc). These form a symbolic Sacred Circle as you journey around the spiral of growth. The path work relates to beginning with the ground of our identity and understanding where we come from. From here we move around the Circle clockwise and gain new insights at each turn of the wheel.

By the end of the journey we have come back to where we began. But this time the Circle transforms into a Spiral because we are able to enter the heart, the Centre.

At the Centre we not only know who we are, but we also can activate the spiritual power inherent within us. By connecting with the energy of the earth, we find ourselves after eons of being lost and without purpose. The skills we learn through the process open capacities for personal fulfilment. We learn pathways of learning, changing our mind, moving forward and healing others and ourselves. Like the stones that cry out even when we are deaf to hear, our lives take on new and rich meaning. Our hands are no longer ordinary hands. We reach out and find ourselves being touched by divine inspiration. We are now connected. In this way we are becoming custodians of the Old Law.

For this activity reflect on where you have come from. Ponder over your personal story. Here are a few questions to consider as you reflect and write in your journal.

- What were the major touchstones along the way?
- Who were the inspiring voices?
- What is yet to be explored in future?
- Where are you now?
- Where do you want to be in five- or ten-years' time?

To honour your thoughts, we recommend that you write in a journal. There are many blank books in bookstores and stationary shops. Even a scribbler will do.

When you find a journal write down your ideas and answers to the questions above. Perhaps review the chapter once more and write down the ideas that spark your interest, questions that come forward as you read, or areas you might like to explore in future.

As journaling is central to spiritual awakening, more suggestions on journaling will be offered as we go along. We have kept a personal spiritual journal since childhood, and we started this discipline during 1978. The practice of self-reflexivity is central to growth in self-awareness whether you do this by journaling or via other types of learning and/or meditation. In your journal, over time as you grow in perspective, you will look at your writing in new ways. This awareness will change you in ways that will surprise and mystify your mind, and perhaps give you a deeper insight from the heart.

We suggest just begin by short notes. Five to ten minutes a day is more than enough for most people to start. Some folks will want to use their phone or tablet to keep notes in a journal. Others will find it easier to use a voice-to-text application.

2 East: Threshold of Manifestation

Eastern Door, sunrise new

Standing waiting open

Entry of sacred inner grove

Eagles standing guard

Guide our quest, free and wild

    Of the mysteries of the spirit there is one truth that comes to me, a truth that we would like to share with you. To receive a blessing from the Great Spirit we are wise to give something of ourselves in return. In the greater scheme of life, reciprocity is a central law that requires respect and action. It is not possible to consciously receive gifts from Creator without opening the mind and heart. Yes, it is true that many gifts are given freely, just as we would give a gift to a child. The child is not necessarily aware of the relational context of the gift, nor might the child consider that some gift might need to be given in return.

    It is also true that when we enter into an adult relationship, we become aware of mutual respect and of giving and receiving. More so, when we enter 'the way of blessing,' it is customary to offer the self in service while asking the Great Spirit to open doors of understanding and insight. Traditionally this act is associated with adult baptism, or when people have already been baptized as children the same transformative life-passage occurs during confirmation. But in everyday ways, these traditional sacraments are part of the past for most people. Initiation into the pathways of spirituality comes to people now in ordinary ways. In this context we recall the older ceremonies for their instructive value. In both adult baptism and confirmation are implied the ancient cultural dimensions of initiation into a way of life that is about giving and receiving and the learning process that both involve.

In other cultures, different forms of initiation are encouraged to help children become adults. Becoming an adult means to take on social responsibilities and relational obligations. We also enter into a spiritual relationship with others and our environment. These initiations open up an awareness of how our lives touch on everything around us, within us, and with the forces of nature that are beyond our immediate awareness. When entering this covenant of mutual relations within the spiritual world people often ask for gifts of protection, insight, knowledge, healing and many other gifts. In our prayer we also give the gift of ourselves to Creator. This gift that we give is the dedication of the self to a path, a way of life.

This form of 'confirmation,' as taking on of social and spiritual commitments, is the first stage in learning to give of the self to others that exists in traditional cultures and remains important to this day. Within this threshold young adults learn that life requires 'give and take' and that often giving is more rewarding than receiving. Within this initiation core values of altruism are encouraged because in giving ourselves to a Higher

Power we take on a deeper responsibility to become a good person in the world. We learn over time how to give.

Giving is but one of the lessons opened up during this early phase of life. The whole experience of our first thresholds of being conceived, born, weaned, eating, crawling, walking, speaking and communicating are associated with the primary layers of self-awareness. During later childhood years we learn to relate to the people around us in complex patterns of communicating, through thousands of verbal, non-verbal and intuitive cues. We are still sorting all this information out at the time we reach the ages of 10 to 13 years, during the traditional time of passage into young adulthood. Within us are also brewing spiritual longings and visions innate to young adult development. If we have the proper sort of encouragement and mentoring, we can understand the importance of awakening spiritually to our life-purpose. As we grow into adulthood, we can more easily relate this need for spiritual awareness to how we create relationships of respect and honour within family, tribe and nation.

Initiation creates a firm foundation for living a rich and full life in society. Having this support is so important. Initiation prepares the spirit for awakening, enabling a young person to undertake the search to find life-purpose, even though simple goals. These processes give a person a sense of place, of belonging. One's most basic loyalties are established by embedding values toward loving, listening, respectfulness, kindness, as well as forming relations based on giving and receiving in fairness. These awakenings become quickly planted in the subconscious of a person but stay with us our whole lives through. Having these experiences during an early age is so important.

For young people to awaken in these ways, the adults in society must also be guided by a spiritual base of awareness. If we did not receive these values early on, as adults we must awaken these longings and find their fulfilment before we can pass them on to others. Side stepping these essentials is where the fabric of initiation has broken down, leaving people in society without a rudder to guide their ship.

People today go all their lives without authentic cultural and spiritual guidance. Along the way people face so many challenges and crisis that could otherwise be avoided. And when they face these times of personal upheaval, their lack of initiation into the basic mysteries of human life leaves them without life-skills to cope. People then lose hope and end up in a mess, and only then might seek help by seeing a counsellor. Professionals will also have no clue about these underlying issues because they also missed out on valuable forms of initiation.

Early experiences of initiation into the basic mysteries of human life give youth a sense of belonging to their family, tribe and nation. This experience protects them from becoming adrift and purposeless. The learning gained provides them with basic life-skills that help them, as they grow older. The orientation also prepares them to know that at some stage they might seek more, and when they do, they will have an idea of where to look for insight and wisdom.

When societies have lost these forms of 'confirmation' and 'initiation,' youth tend to suffer greatly and will get into all manner of mixed-up activities and habits-of-thought. They will not grow up with an innate sense of respect for other people and for elders. Youth without guidance will take three or four decades to grow beyond their confusion. But by then they will have created so much damage in their lives and in the world that they will suffer with post-traumatic stress and other psychological issues. That is, if they succeed in just surviving the growing years.

To understand why this is so important, we need to comprehend how people are made. We can easily understand how human babies need continual love and attention. Why do we think that when children grow older, they can be left to their own devises? Why do we relegate their sacred care to educational systems that are self-serving and quite often do not have the best intentions at heart for our children?

We set children free to roam in an alienating social system and expect them to find their own way through the maze of confusing energies, conflicting messages, and downright misguided values. In ways I am an advocate for a radical transformation of society that involves creating social commons where people can raise children and youth in the context of family, extended and intentionally created family, and local community. I've seen many encouraging examples of home schooling that provide youth with much more direct input into their development as people. We need to explore alternative models while understanding that we can't turn back time, but we can reawaken solutions to these problems that will increase everyone's quality of life.

When we have missed an important developmental milestone along the way, we also need to understand how to address that as adults, so that we can create social programs to assist people to regain a sense of balance. We then need to incorporate this inner need for stability into a life-long attitude of learning and growing towards maturity. One of the keys to opening these pathways is learning to acknowledge one's strengths. In the core of each person is a wealth of resources waiting for silent recognition. In the modern world our minds are clouded. We do not see inwardly without a great effort to overcome the shortcomings of our perception. Part of experiencing reality clearly is found through understanding how our being works. We can pause to explore these issues.

We take in experiences through our five sensory systems and over time form memories and associations to people, places, events and things. Inside of us are ways of operating that include emotional states, personality traits, likes and dislikes and other kinds of dispositions that orient us to the world around us. Gender is one kind of disposition that is partly genetic and partly learned through socialisation. Sexuality is a layer of gender identity that relates to physical, emotional and psychological dispositions to intimacy and sharing of our bodies with another person or persons.

Our psychology is made up of thoughts, emotions, memories, attitudes, beliefs, values and many other aspects that make up our identity. For many years' identity has been my focus of research because I am fascinated by how people make their sense of meaning in life and how they pull themselves together again after major forms of trauma, loss and grief. Identity is a term that expresses the complex nature of human self-awareness. Remember that we began talking about early ways that we grow in awareness from childhood into early adulthood? Identity is something that grows within people since their earliest memories to the present moment.

The daily functioning of people is another fascinating area that feeds into identity over time. Nothing with us humans happens in only a moment. We are born into a context. We grow within relationships. We come to terms with our identity over time. But even in a moment we can have an experience that is life changing. These can be many and varied, including a happy or very sad event that stays with us for many years. As the future becomes today and the past is transformed in the present moment, we live within the eternal now that guides us to who we are already becoming. Our future manifests from what already exists as potential and power within our lives and around us. The past becomes more and more like a story that we can share from a new place of wonder, awe and warning.

Within human beings are also two basic operating systems that interact and overlap. To me this idea comes from a very old First Nation story but is reflected in the teachings of most cultures around the world and appears in modern psychology. The story relates to how an Elder shares with a young person the nature of being human. The teaching is very powerful.

Within every person are two wolves, a white wolf and a black wolf. One wolf is focused on giving of the self to others, learning and remaining open to correction, growing and becoming an influence for peace and healing in the world. The other wolf is focused on taking from others, making assumptions and presuming to know the truth without thinking through the consequences, staying the same without effort to change, and desiring to cause harm and havoc with others.

After the youth hears this story, the Elder turns and looks directly into the eyes of the youth. You also have both these wolves within you. Then there is a long silence… The youth cannot stand the steady gaze of the Elder whose eyes feel like they are examining the very nature of the spirit inside. Then the youth turns away and reflects for a while. When ready, the youth turns to the Elder and says, 'how will I know which wolf is the stronger?'

This is a very important question. It suggests that the youth is having a moment of identity confusion as they realise that inside them is this potential for either way of life. It also suggests the youth is uncertain about their loyalties – what do they want to choose for their own life? This is such an important question that every young adult needs to ask and to consider seriously, because when the question never gets asked people tend to fall into patterns and habits that can lead to places that are not helpful.

The Elder turns to the youth then and say; 'You will know which wolf is the stronger by knowing what wolf you choose to feed.' The answer says a lot. On one hand, we might unintentionally feed the unbalanced wolf and wake up one day and realise we've ended up in a place we never intended. But life is funny that way. Even when we do things we never consciously chose; we still must bear the consequences.

Likewise, we can choose to feed the balanced wolf and at times the unbalanced wolf. Over time we might create our own internal and ongoing confusion, and maybe eventually a form of balance might emerge. It sounds risky. We may also try very hard to feed the white wolf but still end up imbalanced if we also deny the black wolf exists. Denial creates its own forms of energy. There is no absolute right or wrong in this approach to life. There are only choices, and there is what works and what does not work. When we feed the unbalanced wolf, we may also take a certain risk because the story implies that both wolves will become stronger with every feed, and will then desire more food, and the cycle would likely be endless. Once you feed the unbalanced wolf you risk opening the pathway to becoming enmeshed with the darker side of yourself and can easily become confused because your values become divided. Perhaps there is a difference between feeding a wolf and being aware that wolf exists. We are after all more than what we feel. But in the end, the First Nation story stops with the comment of the Elder. The rest is left to us to ponder. And this too is important. In Native culture the point is that every person is responsible for his or her decisions. We each need to live and learn. We can't always learn from others, even our Elders.

We personally need to take the risks and often learn the hard way. So, we try feeding each wolf and see what happens. We can only learn from listening and observing. Sometimes we might not see the outcomes of our actions for quite a while. So, the process is somewhat unpredictable. By the time we wake up to the harm we cause, it might in some ways be too late. But life is like that too. And it is never too late to learn, to change and to grow. We have known many people who awaken on their deathbeds. It might seem too late, but the human spirit is very powerful. In my role as a spiritual mentor these people call me to help their hearts to heal and to let go of old wounds. They tell me their sorrows and say sorry to Creator in their own way. Then they make themselves ready to move on to the spirit world with freedom and peace.

When learning the ways that people's inner being works, it was helpful to understand that all people experience 'core states.' These core states are also in parallel with the white and the black wolf symbolism. There are core states of balance. These include peace, joy, hope, love, ease, contentment, faith, fullness, patience and kindness. These states of awareness are embodied not only in the mind. Core states live within our bodies. They manifest as a complex interaction of our thoughts, feelings and bodily sensations. States of balance thrive when we are in harmony with the environment around us. Harmony arises when we are in healthy relationships with the people in our world. To find these experiences and to manifest them in our daily lives we need to come back to a deep abiding awareness of who we are. When we have lost our way, these states of balance also tend to lessen in frequency and intensity.

Likewise, there are states of imbalance. Core states of being out of balance can sometimes obscure the purity and power within us. Notice how we define these states. We still use the term balance. This suggests that unbalanced states do not have their own existence per se and will tend to dissipate when the person moves back into balance. This principle holds true when considering that the practice of the dark arts of spiritual manipulation works with the illusion of power over the environment and other people. Within this illusion are forms of fear, anxiety, and reactive energies that also dissolve when light enters the shadows. No true spiritual power works in this manner. All true power within creation works in harmony to create life, openness and freedom.

The experience of being out of balance is like feeling the presence of phantoms, they come and go and have no lasting value. Yes, they can be our teachers and as such might have some instructional value, but inherently being out of balance has no value of its own except for how that state leads to a new learning or change of heart. Sadly, those who practice the dark arts of emotional and psychological manipulation may not have the capacity or desire to learn from mistakes, but rather will turn those experiences into even greater reasons to blame anything and anyone but themselves. But the truth remains clear. States of imbalance have no inherent existence apart from being like the shadow. The shadow exists only in relation to the light. Both exist together as two sides of one mystery. But the shadow disappears into the light and gives up its energy to the fullness of being and to creation.

The states of imbalance include experiences of hate, sadness, fear, jealousy, anger, lust, anxiety, despair, envy, vulnerability and powerlessness. Like a mirage on the desert, these states will disappear when we shift slightly and lean toward balance. As soon as one of the states of balance emerges whatever elusive state or complex of states existed within us will tend to dissipate and be replaced by a state of balance. Many people associate these states with health and wellness verses illness and dis-ease. To some extent that makes logical sense. But the danger is that people tend to then assume that certain inner states cause manifestations of health or illness. While I am sure this is part of the picture it is only a part and cannot be confused with the physical development of many forms of illness and disease.

In more extreme cases it is true that there are aspects of these principles we can see in cases of mental health psychosis where the imbalanced wolf has become out of control and tends to dominate a person's way of being in the world. These extremes show us how interwoven our being truly is, because the make-up of our physical and chemical brain has an important part to play in our overall functioning. But for most of us, using the story of the wolves and being aware of our inner states of being balanced or out of balance is enough for us to keep things on the steady. We can work with what we have. When our brain-make-up is basically functional, we can explore our being to a great extent without too much worry.

Part of the safety and security that we need to enter into the inner worlds of our psyche are skills learned over time. In traditional cultures initiation includes basic exercises of strengthening the psyche, heart and spirit so that when in later life 'shit happens' young adults are prepared and can ride the waves of emotional crisis. Sadly, in our day most people in modern societies have not benefited by these traditional lessons. We no longer have the life-skills we need to cope with being human. Therefore, many problems exist in personal and social worlds and society overall faces more unsettling times due to people not having the skills they need to maintain balance.

This being said, we can still learn these skills. It is never too late for learning. Truth be told, life itself tends to throw us into situations where we will sink or swim. All forms of initiation regardless if planned or part of life unfolding have one central purpose. Surrounding the self and deeply connected to the functioning of our mind is that mystery we call will power. Will power is our ability to channel the energies of our emotions towards living within the core states of balance and wellness. All of the central traditional teachings and the whole purpose of all tests of character and initiation are to build the human being's core ability to grow in power.

Will power is one of the most important aspects of being human. By will power we mean the ability to consciously choose a course of action and to manifest one's inner vision or intention in the world. Will power is associated with commitment, strength, ability and capacity to follow through the process of any decision. But will power is also a form of being open to learning and changing, being flexible and considerate to new information as it appears. Power deserves much more time to discuss, but for now, suffice it to say that within every person is the ability to create and to destroy, to manifest balance and to bring about great imbalance. Inside of all people lie the seeds of divine creation as well as mindless destruction.

The path that we begin when we grow in self-awareness leads to many outcomes, but central to human life and development are the spiritual layers of our being that allow us to use the power within us in concert with the environment and world around us. When we take this path well, we come to understand our purpose in life is to help the fabric of existence to sustain all life through our simple acts of kindness, our prayers, our very thought-energy-forms and our way of walking each day that honours the states of balance in all that we do.

By asking the Great Spirit for a life worth living, a life that is grounded within a sense of spiritual peace, we need to recognise that a certain degree of discipline and effort is required to grow each day towards our goal. Regardless what path we choose to take, we will always give of ourselves in some way. If we choose a lesser path, we may give ourselves to various forms of selfishness and greed. If we choose life and more so, if we hear the call towards becoming more than we are now, we may find ourselves giving precious gifts of time and ability to assist other people along their path.

When we live this way for long enough, we may find ourselves manifesting new forms of being that we never thought possible. We may find ourselves taking up a life of dedication to healing and spiritual growth. Deep within the person a form of commitment to intentions of the spirit may arise. When this happens, people become able to move into new vistas of human potential.

This important threshold is expressed through transitions into senior status in community or within a field of work. In cultural and spiritual traditions marriage and commitments to family life are only the first step toward maturity. In later life, as people awaken to a spiritual calling, they may seek forms of ordination to a way of service such as priesthood, ministry or leadership. But in more traditional cultures, ordination happens sometimes spontaneously as the gifts of a person are awakened through some life crisis, major illness, or through a capacity that appears to be given at birth. To be an elder in many aboriginal cultures does not require chronological age.

The qualities of an elder include demonstrating forms of wisdom, kindness, generosity, caring, and service to others as well as an awakening to spiritual life. In the advanced degrees of elder wisdom people consciously embody mystical callings to learn and practice profoundly powerful ways of thought, prayer and higher consciousness. These elders of high degree may grow quite skilled in healing arts, divine arts and ceremonial practices. There are many pathways into the mystery of spirit. Just as there are many spiritual traditions to assist us in living.

All people have an inherent ability to heal their own bodies and to channel healing energy to others. But if you are called to the path of being a healer, to not use your ability may cause the energy that would otherwise flow through you to become blocked in your body. This may lead to illness. The first stepping-stone to taking up the healing path is about preparing yourself as a vessel of healing.

Mi'kmaq Elders teach that we need to become hollow bones through which the wind of Spirit can blow. Only when we are like an empty Ancient Tree, can other creatures come to shelter inside of us. This is one of the teachings that make the native flute a sacred instrument. The hollowed-out piece of wood is rendered sacred by its emptiness. Only when completely unobstructed can the wood become a creature of celestial music. Then the creatures and spirits of life are drawn into the open spaces of creation provided by the hollow bones. The energy we need for healing others and ourselves arises when we empty ourselves of ego and attachments.

We become elders only when we walk the path of selflessness in service to others. Healing then, is about emptying the self of whatever fills us up most of the time, and allowing something else that is purer, truer, and more in-touch with the Life Force around us to fill us up and flow freely through us. Preparing yourself as a vessel of healing is itself a life-long task grounded in dedication while living from a place of vows to compassion, loving kindness, patience, forbearance, forgiveness and cleansing of the self on a daily basis. Inherent in these vows is the commitment to do no harm to others.

The second stepping-stone to becoming a healer is to listen and observe life very closely and carefully. There will be subtle and not so subtle signs that arise, drawing you toward a healing path. Others will see in you a certain potential. Listen to what they say. Learn whatever you can and continue to stay open to whatever Life has for you. Take a humble path. If you are meant to become a healer it will be in spite of you, not because of you. Indeed, you may do all you possibly can to learn and remain open-minded and of good heart, but ultimately the gifts of becoming a healer are given by the Spirit of Life. We can best prepare ourselves by standing aside and by allowing the process to unfold. Try to stay out of the way. Whenever standing in the way of my path I always fell on my face. The key is to get out of the way, and then your path unfolds freely.

The healing path takes many forms. In traditional cultures paths included herbal lore, natural medicine, shamanic vision work, hands-on methods of working with energy, dream-work, and sacred healing ceremony. These methods are alive and well in today's world and are used by many people across cultures.

Hands-on healing is one way. Native North American energetic healing is another. Distance healing arises during higher degrees of skill. Bi location while influencing people from afar is another form of spiritual power. Journey into people's dream worlds is an important form of healing. Entering the World Beneath the Earth allows a healer to engage unconscious, dream, and ancestral earth-bound connections to issues. Moving into the World Above the Earth sometimes involves connecting with people's over-soul that guides their life, or with their familial spirit that forms a collective energy sustaining and guiding their life. In this realm there are also tribal and ancestral powers, angels, protectors, totems and guides. In many ways these forms of work allow for ways to engage trans-generational healing that improves people's current situations, especially where histories of great trauma and hardship are part of a person's current familial inheritance. Others are drawn to more mainstream psychological methods like intellectual healing and cognitive processing that enables people to achieve positive outcomes in life. Still others may be led toward medicine, science, psychology, counselling, and the many therapeutic disciplines like occupational therapy, speech pathology, and massage therapy. The inner desire to become a healer can manifest in hundreds of ways.

How we come to identify with different traditions and forms of meaning is fascinating, and not very simple. Healing is itself a process but is also linked to cultural forms of meaning. For example, certain traditions of Reiki come from Japan and express the energy of that cultural heritage. Likewise, my approach to healing incorporates the energies of the Elders and Sacred Traditions that inspire my work. Therefore, those who engage the paths of healing will eventually need to integrate and form ceremonies that honour the different traditions they respect and uphold. By doing so, the powers and intentions of healing within the traditions are opened for good purpose. Respect is paid and the Ancestral Spirits of each tradition are honoured by the work.

Over the years we have explored many spiritual truths and have come to honour and respect many traditions. In the Sacred Circle work stands in solidarity and respect for many Elders of different cultural ways. In Ceremony we have stood with these Elders and felt their power and listened to their teachings. While celebrating the Christian Mass of Creation composed during the past to honour Mi'kmaq traditional cultural ways, it is natural to celebrate the Sacred Pipe Ceremony given by the Elders. This is conducted during that time of the Mass of Creation when the Body and Blood of Christ is made present and venerated. Upon the altar rest the signs and symbols of Christian, Mi'kmaq, Druidic and many other traditions depending on who is present and what symbols make meaning for them.

Ceremony itself is a natural form of acknowledging the Energy of Life. In this way, we demystify the word, which has taken on many negative associations. There is no doubt that ceremony may involve actual workings within the Energy of Life to facilitate healing, learning or change. But ordinary and everyday ceremony tend to celebrate natural life happenings like the rising of the sun, the setting of the sun, sharing a special meal between friends, and the more special times of life-events like baptism, confirmation, hand-fasting, marriage, ordination, consecration, awakening an elder, or dedicating and cleansing a new home.

Jesus of Nazareth remains a central, pivotal and dynamic part of many people's experience. The term 'Christian' for many people means social and political things in today's world that can be problematic. The most difficult of these realities is that to call oneself a Christian means that you are exclusively only that and nothing else. The way of life proposed in this book is not based in beliefs and dogmas so much as in a process of learning and openness to new expressions of meaning. This pathwork embraces many forms of spiritual and cultural traditions. These may include Mi'kmaq First Nation Medicine; Aboriginal Australian Dreaming; Celtic Druidic Traditions; Goddess Traditions; Oriental Buddhism and Tibetan Buddhism; and the ways of western science, psychology, sociology, counselling psychotherapy, to name a few of the central paths of my life.

The spiritual path invites us to awaken to what means most to each of us. More so, when we say 'yes' at a spiritual level we can find ourselves on the threshold of manifestation where our spiritual nature is called forward. We are challenged to emerge. Our inherent power to change and evolve is awakened. We become the Creator's hands and feet on this planet. We unite with the Spirit of Evolution, and our lives continue to evolve when we are on our path. As such, we are becoming more and more a divine manifestation on earth. The more we bring our lives in line with the core intentions of the Creator, the more we manifest our original purpose. This reflects the energy of the Eastern Door, which is all about new beginnings, the rising of the sun, and the power of the Eagle Medicine Dreaming that protects spiritual young hatchlings.

These ideas are not new. Beings like Jesus, Mohammad and Buddha pointed the way. They did not ask us to worship them as individuals, per se, but to acknowledge their Godlikeness and to take up the challenge of changing our consciousness towards becoming more like them. These prophets call human beings to become aware of our innate capacity to grow in spiritual power and to manifest the Divine Life of Creation in the everyday world.

Regarding these truths, I believe that Indigenous peoples have a profound message for all people on earth. They have lived closer to the 'garden of Eden' spoken of in the creation stories of Jewish history. My own journey to realising Native affinity has taught me that my former Christian beliefs were too closed to the wisdom of other cultures. Many Christians still believe they have the only truth, and that all other spiritual teachings are either just wrong or even satanic. The Holy Spirit wishes us to have greater humility than this belief warrants. There are many paths created by the Holy Spirit through many different cultures and all contain a wealth of truth to assist people on their journey toward manifesting the divine life.

When we began to study Christian history, it became obvious that virtually all of the major sacramental and spiritual symbols were taken from other religions. Many symbols come from ancient indigenous traditions around the world. For example, the symbol of the cross predates Christianity and existed for thousands of years before the time of the Roman occupation of Jerusalem during the lifetime of Jesus. The cross is found in the form of the 'ancient tree' of Celtic spirituality and the 'world-tree' of various indigenous traditions. The Cup of Blessing, and the bread and wine ceremony date back to ancient traditions that surrounded either an altar of stone or a fire and hearth, both incorporated into the Christian symbols. The fire brought into the Pascal Candle, representing the Light of Christ. Baptism and confirmation have many parallels to coming of age initiation ceremonies across most other societies.

As Christianity has spread around the world, it has adopted and assimilated the symbols and traditions of local indigenous and pagan cultures ('pagan' meaning 'of the countryside'). Many churches throughout Europe are built on the site of original shrines to local Gods and Goddesses. In certain locations, these deities were assimilated by changing the stories into those of saints and/or by overlaying stories of the Blessed Virgin in their place. By going beyond Christian teachings a more enriching and meaningful world opens up that points us toward our potential. Human beings are made from many elements of earth; we are all rich in diversity. On one hand we are transcending local and tribal traditions and on the other hand we are rediscovering the innate truths of our tribal origins.

On every front, vast cultural changes are occurring that bring people from diverse parts of the globe closer together. For the first time in human history, a global culture and one global ethic is beginning to emerge that may come to guide the rest of human cultural and spiritual evolution on this planet. This new culture has components both of diversity and unity, difference and oneness, local practical wisdom and universal truth. While we are asked to acknowledge individual and unique gifts, we are also challenged in our day to glimpse a vision of human unity and peace. This vision is grounded in our tribal and racial origins. But also transcends our encoded origins because we are all human and we are spiritual beings who are in some important sense more than the sum of our local identities.

Indeed, the more deeply we enter our local traditions of spiritual insight, the more we are able to vision the world as it truly can be in future. All authentic spiritual practices lead to creating more compassionate, loving and forgiving human beings. Every spiritual path that holds integrity will suggest that, at many turns, a person will need to sacrifice personal gain for a greater good. Yes, there are times to take up arms and fight for justice. But higher spiritual vision always points to actions based in love.

The Native Warrior acts in love. When she or he paints their body for battle they do not paint to intimidate the adversary. They know in their heart that the battle is only transitional, yet another threshold of manifestation that they must pass through to get to the other side of the experience. They know that for whatever reason they are called to act in this way and may need to sacrifice the life of another being during the battle. They know all of this because it was taught to them since they were young children. They know they will need their will power and inner strength because they have already faced many forms of initiation before the day of battle. The Native Warrior paints their body so that they can face their Creator should their own life be sacrificed in battle. They paint their body to honour their Ancestors and All their Relations, knowing full well that they may meet them face to face upon the battlefield of life. They paint their body to be ready to take their journey into the Spirit World. In this way, they accept that their choice to enter the fray comes with many sacrifices of their personal gain and with sober judgment they use their physical and spiritual power with humility.

But it can be just as much a sacrifice to not enter the battle. We remember that most difficult time when we must lay down arms by acknowledging we are powerless to make justice a reality by continuing in the path of war. It was this important insight that guided the decisions of Native and Aboriginal elders who saw the futility of continuing to fight the invasion of Europeans. But the decision to take a more passive path was not weak or based on defeat. A much deeper vision of spiritual and environmental processes guided the acceptance and embrace of Europeans in tribal lands. This vision saw beyond the suffering of the present moment. At the hardest turns of human history, when cultural domination ruled the day, people with deep intuitive insight understood that power is itself a process that ebbs and flows over time.

True power is not to dominate the earth and other cultures. Authentic power shares responsibility and honours the traditions of our Ancestors. As much as European invaders have exercised blind control and power, our European ancestors did not originally teach that such actions are warranted. A greater cultural diversity exists now that arises, paradoxically, from the suffering and wrongs of the past. Today is a time of honouring various traditions, of righting past wrongs and of celebrating and supporting the best in all cultures. The rich wisdom contained in indigenous cultures is taking its rightful place on the world stage.

We are on the threshold of great cultural changes that go beyond any one person's point of view. There are many thresholds, always and forever changing to new heights of manifestation. Part of the mystery of our collective and individual evolution is to realise that we need to manifest what we already are. Instead of compromising our gifts, abilities, insights and cultural wisdom, we need to get in there and share whatever we have to offer. The evolution of human consciousness happens slowly or quickly based on our choices and every person is part of the story of creation.

We each have a story to share. And our stories are our Sacred Medicine. There is much that we need to learn along the way. Our initiations and challenges have a purpose, to lead us forward to become who we already are. In our deepest spirit we have the answers already. The path we take helps us to find that meaning and purpose. Often that path leads us down many winding roads. The journey is the point, because every destination is only another threshold that asks more of us. If we focus on the end point, we lose sight of the valuable lessons we learn today. This is the only time we have. This now is the Sacred Circle of our Being manifest in this skin-time. We need to listen closely to catch the drift.

The following chapters will offer suggestions on how you can bring yourself to new thresholds of growth and personal transformation. While this science is based on an integration of self-psychology, counselling psychotherapy, sociology, historiography, religious studies, philosophy and the newer sciences of physics, transpersonal psychology and a phenomenology of psychic insight, the path and methods suggested herein are simple, direct and applicable to everyday life. This is the power and beauty of being human. We have come to a time in history when the wealth of knowledge around us is so extensive it can take several lifetimes just to read and digest the information. For me, it is enough to focus on the basics that mean the most. You might call this a bit of practical wisdom.

Activity 2:1 Keeping a Journal

After reading this chapter, return to your personal journal to recover your thoughts in a safe place. Your own thoughts, feelings, impressions and ideas are very precious gifts. They are given to you from your inner being to help you find your way in life. To ignore them or overlook them is to dishonour your most precious resource. The Energy of Life makes us with an inner spirit that gives us insight and awareness. The process is very, very simple.

Sit someplace quiet. Focus on your breath. Breathe in and out... In and out...

Allow your breathing to be like an anchor in the storm of thoughts that come and go, come and go. Across the mindscape see your thoughts like clouds that come and go. Observe them while you breathe.

In this quiet place, you can burn some Native herbs like Sage to cleanse your body and mind. Still focusing your intention, listen inwardly and ask your inner being 'what is the most important insight for me right now?' and just listen for what comes up... Give it time. Be patient.

Activity 2:2 Meditation Practice

This exercise is a bit different. A lot of questions are offered to get you thinking about your own history and heritage. The key idea here is to celebrate your own story.

- What do you know of your family heritage? Begin with your parents. Where were they from? Jot down any information or ideas you have at the moment.
- Consider the environment where you live – what are the natural features of the land or water bodies in your region? What is special about them?
- When did your parents or grandparents or their parents move into this region where you live – or are you new to this area?
- Trace your history of place and its relationship to your life story... when did the most significant events of your life happen and where, what location? Write out a short story about your family and personal history.

This is your own form of Sacred Medicine, the threshold that brought you to your present place in life. No story is perfect. Allow yours to be real and don't pay much attention to punctuation and spelling. Remember no one else is going to read this story, unless later on you edit the story a bit and give it to someone.

- After you complete the story, how do you feel about it?
- What questions go unanswered for you?
- If you were to write a new chapter to your life, what would it look like?
- What would you like your life to look like?
- How can you begin to create the life you want?
- One final question: If you had to choose only one central value that means the most to you what would that be? Why would you choose that particular personal value?

3 South: Activating Spiritual Potential

Southern Door, Shield Wolf

Growing, opening, moving

Manifest Life, giving birth

All to dream, to live

Dance with us in clear light of day

There are a great many misunderstandings about the meaning of the words 'spiritual' and 'spirituality.' Our first task is to clarify these words. 'Spirit' literally means 'breath.' Pneuma, the 'breath of life.' Spirit is an inseparable part of all existence. The Spirit of Evolution is ever transforming the earth and human existence is always undergoing change.

'Spirituality' then, is how a person makes meaning based on their experience. In another way, spirituality is how we come to view the 'Spirit of Life' and how we understand the most basic elements of human existence such as air, water, fire, earth and breath. 'Religion,' on the other hand, usually includes a more systematically developed theology that tends to be based on one manifestation, revelation, vision or truth. Spirituality is an area that may include religious based experience but also transcends religion. While everyone could be said to have a form of spirituality, that is, a way of making his or her sense of meaning, not everyone could be said to have a religion.

In this way, spirituality is quite close to having a philosophy of life. The difference is that spirituality names the process by which a person comes to have a philosophy that makes sense of their experience. A philosophy comes later after much personal reflection. Spirituality is more about the actual process as it unfolds. In a classical sense, religion is the exoteric or external manifestation of cultural and theological systems that have grown up over time around the centrality of raw spiritual phenomena. For instance, the person Jesus of Nazareth did not walk around with priests and theologians discussing the merits of personal sacrifice over acts of sacred compassion. He lived a spiritual life, period and full stop. Only centuries later did the rest grow up around the spiritual phenomena that Jesus represented to people and to their culture. In this sense then, spirituality is the esoteric or hidden and personal side of spiritual experience that remains somewhat inductive – requiring a qualitative appreciation for direct, raw and immediate personal phenomena.

What is the experience then? The spiritual experience happens in a personal way through direct encounters with the self, other people, the environment, with animals, in a church or with an entity, power or teacher... Spiritual experience can also be a first-hand 'mystical' entering into the intuitive, psychic and transpersonal components of mind-body capacities. Spirituality can also grow over time to become an orientation to ongoing experience, like a way to orient oneself based in certain dispositions and values. In this case, classical western spirituality suggests that people develop different 'charisms' believed to be a gift from Creator. A charism also describes the spirituality that comes to characterise a person's way of life.

For example, people may value simplicity and quiet in their approach to the spiritual. They might enjoy solitary contemplation, and their charism leads them to create a life based on these values. They may end up becoming solitary mystics in the world. Other people may value these things, but their charism includes silent meditation and acts of social justice. These people have a slightly different charism. And their lifestyle may include working with the Salvation Army or helping out at a soup kitchen, while they may choose to meditate twice per day for twenty minutes.

Others may have really different values, like enjoying loud music and dancing that leads to states of elation. Their charism is no less spiritual. If we actually looked around the world, we would find hundreds of expressions of each charism that describe different lifestyles and forms of spirituality. Charism is a function of the meaning and values that people place on their spiritual experiences. A charism is a personal and social form of expression that codes spiritual experience through certain values. For example, a Franciscan charism places emphasis on caring for nature and creation while living a simple life based in values of poverty of spirit. Jesuit spirituality, on the other hand, tends to highlight the value of intellectual clarity and precision of definitions in articulating and then defending the truth. A Salvation Army charism looks to helping the poor and homeless as basic functions of serving the Divine Life within humanity.

'Mysticism' is the practice of spiritual experience. Like all areas we are exploring, mysticism has both simple and complex manifestations. It is at this point that we must explain one fundamental notion. The discussion that follows is based on a naturalistic understanding of spiritual and mystical experience that accepts spiritual experiences as people describe them. It is important to have an open mind plus a broad framework that allows for accepting and understanding people's diverse experiences. For example, if you are someone who does not believe in a deity, feel free to interpret the ideas in this book as a metaphor of growth. In saying this, I believe that the insights framed by the word 'spirituality' can have wide application to any way of looking at life.

Spiritual belief is not so much about a religious faith in a Higher Power. Rather, spirituality is a logical extension of philosophy. The only way we could come to say this is by living life for many years, exploring spiritual phenomena and later forming a basic philosophy that was based on a logical and balanced interpretation of my experiences and the stories of hundreds of other people that we have been honoured to know. After this, learning of new spiritual experiences makes more sense to me and my framework or philosophy has grown to be more flexible. Not a lot can throw me. In this way, affinity to any one religious idea or manifestation is not absolute. In fact, it appears that in the present day our primary task is to transcend the local beliefs of any one religion or spiritual framework and to envision a broad sweeping ethic of care, concern and stewardship for one another and the earth.

Spirituality serves the purpose of enabling people to form resourceful beliefs. As a counselling psychotherapist our interest is not in the sectarian theology of one view over another. Rather, to assist people to form more resourceful beliefs that open their paths to more opportunities for growth and wellness. Once we step from the realm of spirituality into theology, we leave behind the helpfulness of metaphors. Clarity is lost in the details of only one point of view. By stepping into theology, we begin to build systems of belief that may define and limit how the Higher Power manifests their life amongst us. These beliefs lead to limited dogmas that define social, political and religious boundaries. In these ways, theology is more about the exercise of power over ideas and people's everyday lives. While we know that there is another side to theology that actually explores the deepest of spiritual traditions, this avenue is not open to most people. Likewise, the political functions of religions tend to abuse the work of theologians to support the agenda of priests and functionaries and to ignore and demonize theologians whose ideas challenge the status quo. This dynamic has happened many times during our generation when the creative and pastoral work of many people has been silenced by bishops who control the status quo in their churches.

As suggested above, as a psychotherapist the primary concern is neither religion nor spirituality as an end in itself. The focus is on the process through which people experience healing, development and change. Spirituality is one framework to understand human growth and potential. It is a way of looking at the process of change that applies to almost every area of life. It sensitises to multicultural issues and opens the approach to a therapeutic understanding that honours inter-religious dialogue. With this orientation, we work effectively with people from all different religious and cultural backgrounds.

When spiritual crisis or other phenomena arise, we seek to integrate a seasoned view of the circumstances while suspending judgment – understanding that all spiritual, psychic and transpersonal experiences are possible and are, in the minimum, powerful metaphors of human need as well as suggesting higher levels of insight and potential. The threshold approach presented in this book grows out of this underlying philosophical meaning-making work done through reflecting on spirituality. While this approach is presented through self-development, so as to be applicable to the widest possible audience, the work suggested here can easily be applied within the context of counselling psychotherapy.

To activate our spiritual potential always begins with simple processes. The reason why we begin with stepping-stones is because they allow us to gain a basic understanding of who we are and knowing the self is the beginning of all knowledge. Likewise knowing ourselves within relationships is the only way we come to grow in awareness. No person is an island and no human being can know the self completely apart from others. Our environment is also a huge part of our relational interactions. The world around us is, in many ways, integral to who we are. Being in touch with this reality allows us to know how to live healthy and balanced lives. This is just as important as developing a meaningful spiritual world of understanding.

Spiritual experience is not all about mystical states of release and wonderment. Most spiritual life is about practical everyday actions. A contemplative way of life honours simple tasks, like doing the dishes by hand, washing the floor, cleaning the windows and making a meal for family and friends. The more practical and down to earth we are today, the more we will access an 'indigenous spirituality' that emerges within our lives rather than something we seek to lay on top of our lives to make us feel or look better. This is why almost every major world religion teaches practical methods of prayer and meditation that direct the practitioner into a state of mindfulness. The wisdom inherent in these approaches is seen when we understand that a generally positive environment in mind and body makes it more likely that we will access inner states of peace and contentment or core states of wellness. Nurturing an overall environmental balance makes it more likely that we will grow and change in resourceful ways.

For each person the practice that is needed may be different given the circumstances and developmental path of the individual. Most clients who come forward for counselling are dealing with incredibly complex and difficult situations that have developed over long periods of time. Sorting through the issues often leads to developing simple and strategic changes in one or more areas of life. One of the great mysteries that we have observed is that when we take simple steps to resolve one part of a bigger picture, many of the other aspects of our lives will fall into place. The major need for us is to find the particular part that will make the most difference in the overall picture. This is why many clients seek out various therapists but remain frustrated because they cannot discover what it is that really needs to change. The art of counselling is about finding the part that makes the most difference and often this part appears to be the least significant when looking at the overall problem. For other people learning to manage financial resources can be a major step towards gaining independence and self-empowerment. Others need to find ways to relax and lessen the stress of everyday life. Methods of meditation, prayer, visualisation and physical exercise can assist in these circumstances.

Consciously taking time out to work in the garden can be a very positive step for many people, especially in our current circumstances where so many of the foods that we buy in the supermarket have been genetically modified and contaminated by pesticides and other toxins. Turning off the television can be a major victory for many people. Learning to communicate with the people we live with by sitting at the table with a cup of coffee or tea, perhaps with gentle music in the background and when the television is turned off can be a most positive experience. Leaving the television off during meals is an important part of family communication. In this day and age any less distraction is better under most circumstances. All practical activities can have little or no meaning but when we look at these activities from a spiritual perspective our lives can be so much more enriched. A sense of inner purpose can begin to permeate all of our activities and a deep abiding contentment can slowly seep into our daily lives.

Because the pace of life in modern society is so fast it is so much more important for us to realise that we do not need to be going a hundred percent all the time. Our body, mind and spirit needs time to detoxify and regenerate. Solitude is an important state of being when we allow ourselves to find personal space and take time out for ourselves. Everyone says they never have enough time and that the demands of family and work do not allow for personal time out. In many ways we have created this social climate over the past several generations, because in the past extended families were able to provide an environment where it was more likely for each person to find personal time. Many practical interventions in today's world involve assisting people to actively create strong relationships and friendships that can help support them through these challenges. These practical solutions are inherently spiritual activities that work to build a more balanced lifestyle and a more resourceful human being.

After studying and practicing meditation over the past 20 years, we have come to realise that it is not the only answer. There are many ways to find peace of mind. Spiritual practice for you may tend to be a rich and varied mixture of activities, from meditation to music to painting to gardening to writing to bush walking. Your work also expresses your spirituality. It may have always been this way and for several years during the past you may have struggled in finding your way. At the most significant turning points during the past, you were able to make decisions that allowed you to do the work that is meaningful and important to you. This may have been outside your conscious awareness. Yet life was happening for you, she would hold you up and would not let you fall.

All of life is meant to be a meaningful song and dance. Not even the shadows and darkest rooms of life are meant to be without meaning. The deepest hardships that you have experienced, such as the death of your father or mother, have over time come to represent the moments during your life when you grew the most. Our points of enduring suffering can come to define our sense of identity in the most positive of ways and can often provide a depth of contrast that carves out a three-dimensional aspect to our lives that could never exist without loss. In this classical sense spirituality is about understanding human suffering.

Self-awareness and reflection on our losses, hardships and experiences of suffering can take on a new meaning when we look beyond the shadows. We encourage you to look within your own life to find the things that you already find are helpful and good for you. We also suggest you look at the things that you have not done, activities that you might like to do, and activities that you are avoiding that will be helpful. If you do all of these steps it will become obvious that there are many possibilities in the context of your own circumstances to assist you in becoming a more grounded, healthy and spiritual person.

Presently, beyond the obvious respect for attending to personal loss and suffering, which opens up many avenues for reflection and healing, one of the most important exercises you can do is to take a moment to self-analyse your life, to take stock of what you do and what you do not do. This is a classic and daily-recommended exercise in many religious and spiritual disciplines.

For instance, St Ignatius suggested taking a short amount of time, twenty minutes to half an hour each evening, to examine the day and to listen to your inner being. He called this an examination of conscience. But I like to think of this approach as a more holistic heartfelt attending to life.

Our conscience is the part of us that finds balance between the right and wrong in all actions, allowing us to be aware enough to change our direction accordingly. A lot of people call this the 'still small voice' inside of us that tells us what is right for us, or warns us of something that is not right, even when there is no obvious evidence to tell us why this feeling comes up inside. This is very complex. What one person does may not be right or wrong to the next person, so conscience is very personal. Many people say they need to learn to actually listen to their inner voice, and that they regret times when they overlooked this inner guidance and then something negative or bad happened as a result.

By taking time each night to listen inwardly while reflecting on the events of the day, decisions made, and actions taken, we can 'grow this still small voice' to a place where it becomes easier to listen even during a huge storm. The spiritual warrior is highly tuned to their inner voice. They may never know when a danger might come around the corner, but they will sense the danger before it arrives. This capacity for 'extra-sensory' awareness lives in all of us. Rather than thinking of this ability as outside of the senses, what we are dealing with here is a highly tuned sensory system – an acute awareness – or what we call sensory acuity. After training therapists in sensory acuity, most of what we call psychic ability is in fact a highly tuned perceptive and sensory based awareness. In many ways we can observe, model and teach these skills. If this is true, it means that everyone has heaps of untapped potential for a range of human experiences that we tend to discount as exceptional and beyond our grasp.

Back to the simplicity of listening to the self at night, in truth, this one exercise is the most valuable and important as it provides the basis for every other growth in awareness, sensory ability, and spiritual potential. The best time for this exercise is just before going to bed, when you take your journal into bed, and relax enough to remember the day's events in a peaceful and prayerful way. This is a challenge when you feel upset about the day. Or when you do not have private space, or the discipline is new. But by doing this exercise every night and when you feel good about life, you train your body to relax into whatever you are feeling and let that be. We are more than what we feel. We can observe our thoughts and feelings from a more relaxed and flexible place.

What you write each night is up to the mood of the moment. Sometimes you may not find a peaceful place, and end up writing your discomfort, hurt, pain or disappointment. After many years of doing this exercise we have found that the majority of nights we can find some objective or new perspective, even during the darkest of times.

This capacity to see beyond the present problems of the day will grow over time. Trust your inner light. The key is the prayerful intention to let go of the day and give everything away to the Spirit of Evolution, to God, to Creator, and then allowing your heart to rest for the night, to trust that Life will open new doors and opportunities in the new light of day. You cannot imagine how important this orientation to Life really is until you try living this way.

The results of this nightly exercise do much more than providing you with self-examination. You will be able to surrender to Life the parts of the day that were difficult, and to ask for guidance and direction for the questions that remain unanswered. Regardless whether your belief in Life is just an idea, a metaphor, or a deeply held belief – isn't it nice to feel that we are not alone.

This sense of 'God' is really about the unfolding Spirit of Evolution, the energy of Life around you, the ability to breathe in and out. The nightly exercise helps you to find a sense of awareness that Life will continue to unfold. The sun will rise. A new day will come. And that this is enough – just knowing this. This time assists you in reconciling self to the painful parts of the day and gives you the opportunity to forgive others and to forgive self for misunderstandings.

By recording your thoughts and feelings in your journal you create notes that eventually provide a narrative of change over time. Months later you might read your journal and remember questions that were brought to 'Life' back when. You can see how those questions posed to the Spirit of Life have been answered through other circumstances.

A journal can help you to see patterns over time. For example, you may come to view your moods in new ways as you see the ways you are feeling each day changes over several months, or over different seasons of the year. You might notice that your feelings about a certain relationship change and develop over many months, and even years, and this might help you to understand the relationship more. As you get to know yourself, your spiritual life may open up in new ways. You can easily find yourself changing the ways you believe towards Life around you. Charting these developments provides significant insights that can help you during difficult transitions.

On a more positive note, we tend to take life as a grand adventure and this helps you to reframe the meaning of difficult experiences. Journaling can become like a record of life's adventures, allowing you to look differently at all kinds of experiences as opportunities for learning, opening the heart, challenging the mind, and discovering new forms of awareness.

If you do not have a journal to write in, go online or go out to a shop and buy an inexpensive blank book or scribbler to keep your notes in. There is no better way to chart changes over time and to promote self-discovery and awareness than journaling. When you are ready to reflect and to write in your journal, take a coffee or tea break and enjoy the experience.

There are many other forms of celebrating personal insight and growth. Many people engage with music, some also create and compose songs. Others draw and their lives become expressed through portfolios of artwork. Some prefer to collect the music of others, and many now collect DVD movies. Others enjoy collecting recipe books. In the old times before printing and paper, people collected many symbolic objects that held the memory and stories of particular events. Writing in a journal is a very popular form of holding our insights and reflecting on our growth, and there are hundreds of ways to engage this process.

Activity 3:1 Examination of Conscience

Ask yourself the following questions and record your thoughts in your journal. These are worded in the first person so that you can speak the statements to yourself.

1. What were the three most enjoyable activities I did over the last week or two weeks?

2. How many times did I do each activity in this timeframe?

3. What was it about each activity that I most enjoyed? Why did I enjoy this part so much?

4. What personal value was highlighted by the activity? For example, was the activity feeding my need for love in

relationships, time in nature, time alone, fun time or some other value?

Activity 3:2 Inventory of Daily Life

1. What are three activities that I do on a regular basis are not so helpful for me? (For example, you might consider habits like smoking, overeating, inactivity, arguing, being frustrated or angry, feeling upset or impatient)

2. How many times have I done each of these activities in the last week or two weeks?

3. What is it about each activity that I find un-enjoyable?

4. If I could change this situation overnight, what would I most want to change?

Activity 3:3 Dream List for the Future

1. Create a dream list. Ask yourself, what activities do I want to do in life that I've never done before? Be dreamy in your answers and let the sky be the limit to your dreams. Make a list of up to 10 dream activities.

2. Pick the top three answers that stand out to you as things you want to do the most. For each activity, write out four positive reasons why you want to do each. Don't allow yourself to buy into thoughts about why you can't do the activity, just allow yourself to dream for the moment.

3. Take each of the three activities now and ask yourself, what is it about each activity that speaks to my values in life? What part of me feels more fulfilled when I think about accomplishing each activity? Jot down your reflections.

4. When you have these answers for each activity, realise that it may not matter so much if you actually do each specific activity. The most important thing here is that the part of you that wants to dream becomes more fulfilled in some way.

5. If you cannot realistically see yourself actually doing your dream list, ask the part of you that wants each dream – 'Part of me that wants this dream, what is the positive intention you have for me in wanting this dream?' Continue to ask questions like this and like the ones in the previous exercise above.

6. Finally, 'Part of me that wants this core intention, how can we accomplish the core intention behind this dream?' Record your thoughts as you go.

4 West: Making a Dream Catcher

Western Door, Great Bear

Earth Mother caring for children fair

Welcome our journey,

Keep us safe

Through the dark night of winter

The key to manifesting human potential is making a lasting change. Of course, change is possible. But the most important part is figuring out what is the most important part to alter and to change it forever. Permanent evolution in human consciousness can affect every other development from now until eternity.

Nothing is more important than finding what change is really needed and making that happen. The first step is to understand the nature of human development. The root of all human actions is our psychology. Our psychology is made up of many spheres of influence that overlap and interact in complex organic patterns. These include environment, ecology, capabilities, behaviours, beliefs, values, identity and spirituality.

We are not so much interested in changing any aspect of human experience just to make things easier. When things are going bad, it is often a message we need to listen to, and sometimes it is a better strategy to turn the heat up! One part of making change is, of course, creating healing and regeneration. But making lasting and dynamic change also involves tapping into our deepest discontentment, our experiences of rejection, defeat and failure.

Yes, we often avoid this realisation and might postpone facing these things for years. But ultimately, we want to face our reality head on. This is the only way to grow into our full potential. We cannot always walk through life pleasing other people or being a slave to our own ego. We are most interested in creating changes that are connected to people's deepest and most enduring dreams. If we can touch and hold on to our core dreams, we have a great power to harness.

We need to develop a driving power that motivates change. Getting disturbed about the way things are is the first step. Reality therapy looks square into what we dislike about today's experience. A bit drastic, you say. It is a most fascinating fact that people will rarely make big changes in their lives until a major crisis happens. We often need a bit of fire under our bums to get moving! It is sometimes easier to initiate change while increasing our sense of being empowered to manage rather than waiting in complacency for change to be forced on us from outside. We do not have to wait for a major crisis before we begin the journey of self-actualisation.

Reality is, all of us are currently in a crisis on many fronts, environmentally, socially, in areas of health, illness, toxicity and psychologically. The only inconsistency is that many of us are not aware of the crisis yet. In almost all areas, human beings are clearly facing the most pervasive challenges that have ever come forward in history. But maybe in your private life you are not in crisis. If this is so, great! You are starting from a position of resourcefulness.

Regardless where you begin, from any point along the path down to the lowest places of powerlessness, defeat and loss created by addiction or violence, it does not matter where you are. What matters the most is where you want to go.

When you want to go somewhere, you can imagine going there and what it might be like. You create a mental picture, sound and body feeling and associations that becomes a symbol of the future hope. The image chosen to represent this chapter is the dream catcher because it represents a fullness and oneness that is found in our dreams, in the circular form of the symbol and in its spiritual and cultural significance.

A dream catcher is a First Nations symbol and tool for personal healing and spirituality. The dream catcher is hung above the place where a person sleeps and when bad dreams come up, they are caught in the web of the catcher. At sunrise, the bad dreams are transformed and dispelled back into the environment. When we made our first dream catcher, we used whatever materials were at hand. Yarn, a metal clothing hanger, beads, one special stone bead for the centre and feathers that were collected over many moons that were gifts from the birds of the air.

The dream catcher is also a symbol of creating good dreams and making changes that will last forever. It is a sign of being able to change and to manifest these changes in life. It links the conscious world of daytime, clarity and insight with the unconscious realm of night, sleep and dreaming. It acknowledges that dreams are something quite mysterious. They come to us and emerge within us during our sleeping hours. Something we cannot consciously control.

The symbol also speaks of the love and care of the Creator, who gives us tools like the dream catcher to purify, detoxify and replenish our spirits within the cycles and seasons of nature. Just as our bodies need time to rest and recover from processes of digestion and sickness, so our minds and spirits need cleansing on a daily basis. At many turns along our path of life we may be drawn to different signs and symbols for making the changes that are necessary. Often the deeper meaning or significance of these symbols may remain hidden from conscious awareness. Only later do certain insights dawn on us and clarity emerges in our consciousness.

Spiritual images, signs, markers and sacraments can open doors to a mysterious world of potential that always lies just ahead of our most recent realisation. These gifts that we are given by others or find ourselves, like simple seashells, lovely jewellery or exotic bush nuts and humble pinecones are all spiritual communications from Creator that speak of the loving care of the universe active in our lives.

All gifts, even our homes and land, are only given to us for a brief time because everything belongs to the Creator. We are often called by life to give what we have, to let go of precious and valued symbols, because in giving we exercise a much more profound freedom from attachment linked to selfishness, control and the pride of ownership. We have often wondered why more people do not exercise a kind of radical detachment from possessions, signs and symbols that make up so much of daily life. The practice of detachment has vastly improved our life beyond measure.

Each of us is really a living, walking, breathing dream catcher. When our mind shifts, the sun and fresh air brake in and our bad dreams are transformed and dispelled. Consciousness is an amazing and mysterious process. Have you ever realised that all the cells in our body regenerate over a period of seven years? Why don't people also think that our minds regenerate and change? Many people believe they stay the same in their personality and mindset for their whole lives.

Reality is, people are changing every day. Though we all have pre-set hardware that was given to us by Life when we were born, we also have the potential of changing and upgrading our operating systems and software at any time we wish. Mindfulness, contemplation, learning, conscious breathing, meditation, prayer and ceremony are the established pathways of transforming consciousness. We have all been given faith, hope and love in our built-in hardware. These practices activate that hardware once we are able to find our 'activation key.'

We can remember the early years of practicing meditation and prayer – there were days when it seemed laborious and boring! Only periodically a glimmer of light and hope would manifest inside me, through a dream or realisation. Small awakenings were given to keep me motivated. But inwardly, the sense that my practice was right and would lead to peace of mind was enough for me to continue through the dry times. Later in life we might not practice exactly the same processes, but the lessons learned stayed with us and have been extremely valuable.

These inner teachings provide wealth and wonder in a world made ordinary and one dimensional. Giving people a way to expand the mind and heart is actually an essential survival skill in today's world. We all need more imagination and creativity, as these provide the resilience and fortitude we need when the chips are down.

We could choose to build a dream catcher in the world. If we did, wouldn't it be neat to make an environment where people really want to belong? A world where people are happy and fulfilled? A world where every person is able to realise his or her potential by living in a peaceful, nurturing society? This dream certainly presents a high standard for action.

The reality of most people's lives is that our standards are created by the expectations of our peer group. It is not easy for any person to maintain standards and goals that raise the heat on an ongoing basis. Over time, who you live with will in many ways be who you become. But conversely, many people come to crossroads in their lives when they decide to make a lasting change and reach beyond their relationships to become a better person, to follow their dream. Ultimately, we are each responsible for our own destiny.

In the process of life, we need to create an environment where lasting change can be nurtured over the long term. Not only do we need to challenge our limiting beliefs, we also need to do a lot of spirit searching to understand our core values in life. We can change our capability in many ways through education, training and work experience. But if our beliefs are limiting and our values are in a mess we will not succeed in the long term. Beliefs, values, behaviour and our environment need to be brought into alignment with our capabilities and all of these parts of our experience need to be grounded in our spiritual assurance that Life, God, the Great Spirit or whatever we call the Higher Power will carry us forward regardless the circumstances. Of course, we will fall on our face from time to time, but the Power of Life will not let us be crushed beyond repair.

Try believing this: Failure does not exist. Only learning exists. The process of learning is the larger picture, the overall dynamic of change. But what we call failure is a small part of the big picture. Failure is only a nasty word for when something does not work. Learning what doesn't work in life is just as important as learning what does work. In the wider scheme of things to build our dream we need to know both.

So, if you see your life up on the big screen in 3-D, imagine your overall goals in life to be clear and beautiful and inspiring. See them on the screen as your life is flowing freely into more and more blessings. Be in that place of living your dream. When you look back on how you came to this place of accomplishing your dream you will see a long string of stunningly beautiful "little failures" all along the way. Now and then, a success will shine out like a star that gave you hope and courage. But when you see the big picture, you will realise that the best practice is to welcome failures just as much as successes. As you look closely, notice how the beautiful little failures provide the very stepping-stones that made your success possible. Allow a deep thankful heart to fill you for each and every lesson learned along the way.

Franchesca Cabrini was an American woman who lived during the years of consolidating the infrastructures of the Eastern States of America. Those were really hard days when people had little access to health care, and when they lived close to a harsh climate and difficult lifestyles. She had a vision of people getting what they needed when they needed it, and in places where they would not have to give up their work and lifesavings to travel hundreds of miles to get medical help.

Franchesca was an amazing women and full of energy and determination. She founded numerous hospitals and public charities all along the Eastern side of America. She once said that when we are doing God's will and working toward our dream, if things are going smoothly something must be wrong. She said that when we are following our dream, we would encounter the most resistance and challenge. This is truly revolutionary thinking. She said this was the case because when we are making valuable changes to the course of our lives and to those of others, we are actually asking the Spirit of Life to provide us with enough resistance to make us stronger.

When we are working towards our goals in life the Higher Power will give us roadblocks and difficulties to teach us vital lessons. Otherwise there would be little challenge in manifesting a dream or vision of change. She taught that nothing is too great or heavy for the children of Creator. The more we open ourselves to God's dreaming our lives instead of us believing our dreams are the right way to go, the more we will accept the challenges we face as divine guidance and encouragement. What a stunning reframe of life's challenges! And she lived long before the advent of modern counselling psychotherapy.

Yes of course, sometimes we need to admit that roadblocks force us to stop and wait, and sometimes force us to take a path away from our dream. But there is no doubt that many of the daily challenges we face are given to us as signs that we are actually on the right track. But do remember – to feel this energy of 'right path' you first need to find your path. Once you do, look out. Things will not get easier! But you will be given the strength you need to live your life purpose. And let me tell you, that is an incredibly rewarding and exciting experience. There is nothing more satisfying that knowing without any doubt that you are on the right path, doing what you are meant to do in life. In this way, spirituality represents the fullness and balance of the whole person who knows the meaning of their life and is living within their sense of purpose and mission.

The question is asked, how can people discern between our personal dreams and the dreams of the Creator for our lives? How can we know we are on the right path? In traditional western mystical teachings, 'discernment of spirits' is a process that the novice learns over several years. These processes involve learning to quiet the mind while listening to the heart and opening up spiritual levels of perception or what modern psychology might call higher levels of consciousness that enable a 'bird's eye view' of the 'bigger picture' of life. Discernment also involves attending to emotional patterns over time, listening to personal challenges, learning from personal weaknesses and dispositions, and becoming increasingly honest and transparent within the self.

By coming to terms with yourself you can find the Great Spirit's intentions for your life. Traditional cultural ways suggest that the Creator encodes within us an innate mirror of divine life. We first need to become self-aware to know the mind of the Creator. Across many cultures the indications are similar, and may include learning the ways of the culture, traditions, ceremonies, and meanings associated with creation and ecology. In First Nation traditional ways, the Creator speaks directly and often symbolically to us through various means including dreams, visions, the teachings of Elders and in the voice of creation and ecology.

Can you get a glimpse now of why change is a permanent process when we are on the path of personal evolution? If all the parts of a person's life are brought into alignment their momentum for change actually accelerates. They literally vibrate at a higher frequency, and the movement of the spiral dance of evolution flows freely. So maybe we are the Goddess's dream catcher and the Creator dreams us each and every day.

Great Spirit's good dreams are realised and the bad dreams that awaken within us are merely parts of us that are asking for help, sometimes crying out for assistance. Maybe these are parts of the Creator that are still being created, still emerging, caught in that painful cycle of birthing newness and creativity.

When we awaken from a bad dream, maybe the God of our Ancestors comes alive again and we walk, act and become today what was dreamed of hundreds of years before. If we are the Creator's hands and feet in the world, maybe we are also the Dream of the Divine Being becoming reality… as the future becomes today, and the past is transformed in the present moment.

Perhaps we can learn how to create a dream catcher in our bodies, and then sort through our dark dreams while coming to celebrate and embrace our good dreams. Accessing our dreams of hope, faith and love is a part of our purification. To be purified is to dream the dream of light, that which will dispel our most invasive darkness. To live within this dream, we often need to face our demons. When we embrace our weaknesses in faith, they can become our greatest strengths.

Many clients we work with seek to understand their boundaries and to become empowered to change after having survived violation, and while still feeling crushed and disempowered. Many women that come forward have experienced abuse and trauma and are looking for a new way of experiencing personal safety and wellbeing. In many of these cases we have taught people to open their own sacred space and thus to reclaim their boundaries and sense of personal power.

The process involves giving people an immediate and positive experience of safety, empowerment and the ability to do personal healing work. Once these skills are imparted a lasting and permanent change is created by which people can move on with their lives in more resourceful ways. These mind-body strategies are extremely powerful in breaking the spirits that bind people's lives; spirits of fear, domination, anxiety, depression and powerlessness created over years of living in relationships that promote self-denial and enmeshment.

The human spirit needs to live in an environment that is free from the spirits that bind happiness and growth. The Creator wishes a dream of goodness to awaken in each and every person, and our time to wake up is now. The following exercise is designed for anyone interested in exploring personal empowerment, dreaming and creative visualisation aimed at releasing our lives from the spirits that bind us.

The new freedom we experience must be grounded in our truest being, our Self, created in God. And the empty spaces left open after our changes can be filled with the Great Spirit's dreaming of our lives. It is not enough to change something in our lives, to let go of a behaviour for instance. We need to find something new, to learn a new skill, to flex our abilities in a new area, to act in new and more resourceful ways. This is acting as children beloved and cherished by a Creator who is still intimately involved in our lives.

Plan to do this exercise when you have from 30 minutes to an hour alone. If you need to wake early, before the children and family are up and about, this may be a good time to find solitude and quiet. It is also a time when most of the world still sleeps and the energies of the day have not yet awakened into full swing. Some of our best moments for prayer and meditation, times when the spirit feels most rejuvenated, are during the early hours of morning between four and seven. This is not surprising as many monastic traditions dedicate the early morning hours to prayer before sunrise to awakening the human spirit through contemplation. Many farmers in the bush tell a similar story that when they are out for an early morning ride on the land, all is as it should be. Aboriginal traditions around the world also tend to place strong emphasis on early morning ceremonies. The Mi'kmaq nation in north eastern North America conduct Sunrise Ceremony and hold this as one of the most sacred tasks of the nation to greet the Dawn as it first touches the continent.

If rising early is not possible for you, find an hour in the evening alone. You will need to have the home to yourself and you may wish to take this exercise out into the garden or into a park or natural setting. My early experiences of exploring this exercise were within the confines of familiar walls of safety. This provided me with less distraction because my mind can wander easily, so having a quiet and familiar spot to explore this world of personal space was most helpful.

Many clients have needed to explore this exercise initially within the safety of the therapeutic relationship. Later they have taken it home and expanded on the skills learned in counselling.

But you are free to explore this activity any time you wish, understanding that to gain deeper insight and openness to growth in the Self we need to create an environment where we can nurture the process of resourceful change. While the exercise that follows is related to certain cultural traditions, the process itself in psychotherapy is based in an understanding of the psychobiology of mind-body healing.

However, there is not necessarily any cultural, spiritual or formal meaning that must be placed on the exercise and it can be open to any interpretation from any perspective. We use the metaphors of native ways only as one example of a frame of reference to understand the experience. However, there are just as many significant references to Christian meanings, and to Buddhist, Hindu, Islam, and many other faith traditions that could apply.

In the days leading up to this activity gather together various symbols that will assist you during your hour of personal awakening. You will need between four to eight stones to mark the space on the floor. Personally, we prefer to keep these markers organic objects and to honour the tradition of acknowledging that river stones are song-lines to our Ancestors. We have often borrowed stones from the ocean as well for this exercise in creating personal space.

Stones naturally mark spaces in nature, and you can take time out to find special stones that speak to your spirit. You may one day have two or more sets of stones for different purposes. Stones protect sacred sites and many Aboriginal and First

Nations places of power are conducted where stones mark the place. In Christian heritage, stones are also held as very sacred.

The stone where Jesus wept in the Garden during his passion is still venerated, and once I was deeply honoured to kneel in that very spot and to celebrate the Mass in that sacred garden. Likewise, the stone where Jesus was laid within the tomb in Jerusalem is now protected within a small structure where pilgrims can bend low to enter, kneel and touch the gravestone that held the body of Jesus. At one time of my life I spent an overnight in vigil at that very place, and the experience transformed my life in quite profound ways.

Stones were so important in Christian spiritual experience and theology that every altar throughout history was preferably made from stone and was consecrated with the four elements through the use of sacred salt, water, smoke and fire, and was connected spiritually to the Body of Christ by making a secret chamber inside of the stone altar that kept safe a relic of a saint or holy person known to have lived and died within the grace of the Holy Spirit.

Our Ancestors lived in stone caves across the world and in Europe, North America and in Australia. Many modern homes have stone and brick fireplaces, another symbol of the inner hearth and home of the spirit that protects and directs energy of light and fire, symbols of burning away impurities, growth and regeneration.

In the Native way there is no Mecca or Jerusalem to which people direct their attention. All of Mother Earth is sacred and the attention is pointed inward to the heart and outward to the environment around us. The object of devotion is not obedience to written teachings, nor is it meditation on the truths of particular revelations of God. We can learn from this wisdom to have an open heart and mind, even while we may indeed honour and hold dear personal beliefs that are held strongly and that guide our lives.

Spiritual practice, in a paradoxical sense, is meant to maintain right and healthy relationships with our environment, tribe and society. We do Ceremony to keep us on track, and to remind us of what is important in life. The Creator does not necessarily need our efforts. Yet the process of spiritual practice appears to open and sustain communication between people and the Spirit of Life. Most of the Old Ways of native people acknowledge our ancient role as Custodians of the Land and Sea. This role suggests that maybe Life does need us as much as we need Life.

When individuals take up the spiritual quest for insight and vision, there are specific practices and purposes that grow from this commitment that come to define action that celebrate the meaning of life. We call these ceremonies. One kind of ceremony celebrates or commemorates what already exists. Another kind opens intentions and prayers for what could become manifest in future.

In a more general sense, whenever we have a question, we enter into a process to find the answers. The spiritual quest is the same. Our question may be to find the purpose of our life. So, we set out seeking, looking, listening and waiting for the answer to emerge. When we see something that needs changing, we can also put so much concentration into that action that it comes to be in reality. The second kind of ceremony is powerful in that way, because it enables a special, safe and concentrated place in which change can be considered and focused much like a magnifying glass focuses the light of the sun on one point that can become so hot it may burn whatever it touches. Ceremonial space provides just such a place where people focus the energies of the elements to manifest some intention.

In a similar way the therapeutic space is focused by use of the therapeutic relationship. The focus on personal change and transformation provides a modern container for the intentions of the heart and spirit. Most people today have little patience for these matters, but in the realm of spiritual insight we can never rush the process or demand answers to come to us. The most fundamental value in this path is learning respect, to respect our own spirit, the spirits of our elders, friends and family, and to respect our Ancestors and the Earth who give us gifts of insight when we are ready – not when we want them. This being true, over time the specific answers do come. And each action and symbol used in ritual and ceremony has a range of meanings and purposes.

We can never expect a gift, like a child that wants a new toy we can live in hope but the actual choice to get the toy is not made by the child. Only their parents or guardian can make that choice, which must also take into consideration things the child has no real awareness about like financial situations, budgets and upcoming needs for other purchases in the home. In the same way, the Spirit of Evolution wants to give good gifts to us, but even the Creation must take some time to think, ponder and decide what gift is the best for us as well as how, when and where to give that gift. Even more so, Life may be aware of how we actually will respond and whether we are indeed ready for the greater responsibility that usually comes with spiritual gifts.

Another funny realisation is that many of the most important insights and spiritual gifts that people receive are not about the Higher Power; they are related to our need to learn about ourselves. So, seeking insight in the spiritual realms is a tricky business because first we need to understand our own hearts and minds. This is no easy task! Yet the best of Native traditions teaches us to seek out time and space for our self so that we can learn who we are; because if we go through life not knowing ourselves, we will probably mess up other people's lives too. Native spirituality teaches us ways and means to build strong relationships with our self and others and with creation around us.

Likewise, the Western Christian mystical tradition teaches similar truths. Taking time out for personal prayer, meditation and renewal are core values in this tradition. Finding and building strong personal space through ritual practice stands as a complement and support to Christian action in the world. Christian churches are structures that are built as practical spaces of worship and also as symbols of sacred space. The four directions of the compass, the four points of the cross and the circle of life are integral parts of every traditional church design. These symbols are also part of the mystical awareness and practice taught as a necessary step toward living in the Presence of Manifest Power. During every Christian ceremony even in the most sparse and simple of church interiors, there are parallels to the process shared here with how people enter into prayer within a sanctuary of the church. All these methods, signs and symbols are directed towards our finding union with our Life Purpose and creating a nurturing space where we are more able to manifest divine life on earth, in our lives and in our relationships.

When you have found the special stones, you wish to use in your ritual of finding personal space and you have set aside the time and place for doing the following exercise, you are ready to proceed. For the purpose of this exercise, you are not asked to find or bring any other symbols into the activity. The main symbol of course is you and this process is designed to open up the possibility of gaining new awareness of your own personhood, humanity and energy. Like other activities in this text, this one below is in different parts. Here in particular it might be helpful for you to read through all the parts first before beginning. Once you have a sense of where things are going, you will enjoy your experience much more.

Please, be aware and respect your own beliefs. The process suggested can easily respect and honour many other beliefs and cultural practices. When we use this exercise in therapy the language reflects the beliefs and values of the client regardless what tradition they come from.

The main symbol used is the Sacred Circle. This is a profoundly important ceremonial and cultural space within all the major world religious traditions, as well as for the world's Indigenous traditions. The Circle has its geophysical and mystical importance within ancient European cultural paths including Celtic, Druidic, and Teutonic and in other Goddess based cultures such as those of ancient France.

We might add that the circle is also quite significant from a western scientific perspective as a construct within mathematics, physics, and biology. The circle is important in social sciences, psychology and in economics. Circles also translate into the multidimensional processes of spirals, and these open up the quantum fields of time-space dimensions.

Within circles and spirals human beings have an innate awareness of potential, power, movement, evolution, and communication.

Likewise, this activity can be a very simple personal experience not linked to wider beliefs at all. Indeed, we have used this activity within psychotherapy over many years and while acknowledging and respecting the beliefs of the client, the actual process itself is quite pure in that it does not have to be based in any beliefs or theological understandings.

Activity 4:1 Collecting Stones

As suggested above, place the stones in one location in the room or wherever you choose to enter into this activity. Remember that in the traditional indigenous way river stones represent our Ancestors and especially those Ancient Ones who inspired the creation of our families and ways of life. Paying respect in symbolic ways is integral to native spiritual ways. And while it may seem childlike and poetic on one hand, the practice of paying respect through demonstrating humility is actually one of the chief methods of opening our heart and mind to new energy, change, insight and power.

This process effectively helps to cleanse our being while opening us to new things coming into our lives. In this way, say a simple thank you to each stone and place them in whatever spots you choose that will form a circle that is just outside the stretch of your arms when turning around and reaching out from side to side. Place the stones around with a sense of respect. Also be aware of the general directions of North, East, South and West for later on in the activity. Although, for this part of the exercise the stones do not need to be placed in these cardinal directions.

Bring yourself to a place of sitting or standing, where you feel most comfortable and where there is space all around you. Move your arms outward around you, sensing in your body and mind the space that is around your body. Speak softly to yourself, 'This is my space, thank you Creator for this space.' Sense inwardly the space that exists directly next to your skin. This is your most intimate space. Reclaim this space as your own, a place where you can invite someone in if you want to, but a space that is uniquely your own. This inner space next to your skin is sacred and powerful. In the spiritual realm, this space cannot be violated by anyone because our bodies are indeed the resting place of the Great Spirit. This means that in the spiritual world, our bodies are Sacred Space. This means that the very energy that created the cosmos exists and lives within our bodies.

Have you ever wondered why people feel so terribly violated when they have been physically or sexually abused? Part of the reason for the depth of pain caused by this violation rests with the fact that we are spiritual beings living within sacred bodies. Our being is so deeply sacred we need to have this inner sanctuary respected.

The space next to your body is your God/Goddess given right to integrity, personal responsibility, and pride in the Creator's creation. In this sense pride is very close to humility, because at once we know we are created in the image of God and yet we know we are humble creatures with so much to learn. In the Circle you stand with the Creator of Life.

If you have ever experienced violation of your most personal space, acknowledge this now. For some this is huge and so, please take your time. Also, be aware if your trauma is heavy. You will want to postpone acknowledging the depth of your pain until such a time as you feel stronger and when you understand and have experience of the empowering processes being shared here. Trust me, I have walked alongside so many people recovering from extreme trauma. They eventually find strength and peace, and this learning process helps them enormously over a six-month period of time to regain their sense of integrity of self.

Consider finding a therapist to walk with you through this process. When working with women who have experienced rape or sexual abuse, this Ceremony of Empowerment can take several hours and cannot be rushed. In these times we respect the person's space and maintain a respectful distance from the Sacred Circle. If you have experienced some kind of violation and you want to explore this exercise on your own, it may be wise to tell a trusted friend when and where you will do this and ask them the favour of being available to call and come to spend time with you if you really need some support.

At this early stage call to mind that no violation can continue forever. Every worst test we endure must end and our lives will continue, and we will learn from the experience. Eventually we find new perspectives and can look back at the trauma without the intensity of debilitating feelings. In our core identity beyond any hardship we have survived, we are first and foremost children of the Creation.

Reclaim your body and physical space as your own. This space the Goddess gave you when you were born. You carry this space with you all your life. It is something that is yours forever. No violation can erase that created by the Energy of Life. As you get to know this personal space again, imagine yourself really and deeply accepting the presence of the Creator in who you are within this space, in your body, inside of you. Breathe in and out and feel this energy flowing through you. Ask yourself as you become more aware of your body, 'what energies have I allowed into my personal space in past?' Take your hands now and gently, slowly, with each exhale, brush the air just above your skin and wash your energy field with the Grace and Love of the Great Spirit.

Accept that within you is a great potential for channelling the energy of divine life and healing. Feel this energy within you now and as you breathe be aware that your breath itself is a healing energy that flows in you and around you. Cleanse your body with the energy of life. This is also your birth right to use this healing energy, and to reclaim this ability and capacity to work with healing energy.

When you have cleansed your body in this simple manner, now it is time to cleanse the space around your inner energy field. Move your hands in a swishing motion through the air around you. As you do this, say calmly with each breath, 'I acknowledge that God/Goddess/Creator… allows me to have this space and it is Sacred. I cleanse this space in the name of the Creator of Life and give thanks that no unwelcome spirits can enter here without my conscious and expressed permission. I claim this space as a place of ritual and healing work, for my own good and the good of those I love.' Cleanse the space and then take a deep breath.

Look around you and sense how your energy continues out from your body. Reclaim this space as well and understand that your basic energy field goes as far as the tips of your fingers when your arms and hands are fully extended. Feel this space. Move around in the space. See, listen, touch and feel what this space is like for you. This is your gift from your Creator.

Just beyond the tips of your fingers is another space that is uniquely yours as well. This is the space where outside energies can come to 'knock on your door' and ask to come in. The choice is always yours. Most women are socialised to automatically open their space to take care of men. While not absolute, this gender socialisation is common. Men on the other hand are socialised to push people away and to use their energy field to fend off predators. This instinct has translated into men being socially awkward and defensive of their bodies, emotional selves and their families.

Take a moment to think about how your unconscious family upbringing influenced how you instinctively use your energy field. Do you invite people in all the time to take care of them? Do you push people away when they get too close? Do you keep people at bay and never really get to know them? Or do you accept people as they are and feel more relaxed about sharing space when and if that happens? Every approach is neither good nor bad, it just is the way we were programmed. Once we are aware, we have more choices. We can then explore new uses of our personal energy and space.

Be aware now that your space forms a complete circle around your body, in all directions, above you and below you. No one can enter without your permission. Imagine you are standing or sitting in a large bubble, this is your own protective membrane and is your birth right as a child of Creation. Extend your arms and palms outward and claim this space all around you. You can open this space any time you wish, through a small door or by completely dispelling the boundary. Your boundaries are your own to command. Clap your hands several times to release the energy. Awaken your sleeping spirit. Take a deep breath. This ends the first part of the activity. You may wish to stop here. If so gather up the stones and close the circle while giving thanks for the experience.

Activity 4:2 Opening the Sacred Circle

Open a Circle with your arms, pointing to the edge that you see in your mind's eye. Look over to wherever your stones sit. If they are inside your energy field, this is fine. If they are outside, be aware of this and gently open a symbolic 'door' to your space and bring in all the stones. If you had placed some stones to make a circle, gather them up now with the others. Sit them all at your feet.

When they are all at your feet, take up one stone. Lift it up level to your heart and face the direction of East. Say a short prayer of thanks to the Creator, whatever comes up in your heart. Place the stone at the outer edge of your circle facing East. Take up another stone and face South. Offer an intention at each turn and place the stones for the four major directions of East, South, West and North. Visualise your circle becoming stronger as you go. Sometimes it helps to visualise a fire burning tall at each direction that extends around the circle. Place the rest of your stones between the others to form the edges of the circle and keep one stone for the centre. This stone will be your 'heart stone.' This stone can sit in front of you as you stand or sit in the circle.

For Christians the heart stone represents Jesus of Nazareth, and in many ways the altar of sacrifice or the cross upon which Jesus gave his life freely so that others could live. The altar stone is the place of gathering of the faithful, who commemorate in sacred memory the gift given with open heart. Because we are believed to be the body of Christ, we too become participants in the living sacrifice of the Son of God. In this way we step into the sacred mysteries.

In a different and even older tradition, the native way places a rectangular stone altar outside of the Sweat Lodge. The stone is placed mid-way between the Sacred Fire and the Lodge. This altar stone is where participants who enter the Sweat Lodge may place person items, they wish to let go of during the Ceremony. They may also place gifts or symbols of their loved ones and of the people or other beings they pray for. The stone represents letting go and preparing your mind and heart to be freed of all hindrance.

In a similar way, when the round river stones who are our Ancestral Spirits are placed into the Fire they are heated and made ready through the burning of sacred herbs such as Sweet Grass, Sage, Cedar and Tobacco. When the Lodge is ready to receive the Ancestors, they are carefully carried into the centre of the Lodge and placed in a hollowed impression that was dug into the ground in the heart of the Sweat Lodge. Upon these stones are poured water that evaporates to make the heat and sweat effective. Here again our bodies become a living altar of sacrifice through time spent in prayer within the Lodge.

Joseph Randolph Bowers

Now to complete the directions of the circle, be aware of the energies of the Sky above and the Earth below. Sense the energies of the original custodians of the land. Give thanks to Creator for these Ancient Spirits and for their living descendants and thank them for the honour of being in this Place. Imagine a taproot extending from your spine down deep into the earth; breathe in the pure energy of the earth. Raise your arms and hands upward and feel the energy rising through you until it gushes up through your spine and nervous system, up and outward, overflowing through your fingers and the top of your head. Connect this energy with the energy of the sky, and after a couple of deep breaths, take down within you the energy of the sky to connect with the earth. Allow this energy to flow through you, down through your spine and into the earth. Feel these two distinct energies intermingle. Breathe through your awareness, deepening your sense of honouring and respecting the insights and truths of your Sacred Space.

The seventh direction is centre. This is your heart. Bring your hands over your heart and feel the energy of the whole circle coming inward and flooding your being. Then imagine the energy overflowing outward from your deep inner world. There are no hidden places in Sacred Ceremony because the whole purpose of the process is to open and cleanse the communication system. By doing this again and again, the Ceremony purifies the body and spirit.

Give thanks for the energy of your heart and know that God has always dwelled there with you, even when you least felt the Creator's presence. Invite the energy of the Holy Spirit your Creator into your heart to cleanse and purify your being. If you do not believe in a deity or if metaphors of divine beings makes you uncomfortable, simply think about the powerful natural energies of the earth and of the spirit or energy hidden in evolutionary time, that creative and amazing force that formed the mountains, the seas, the green life and all creatures that evolved on the land and in the depths of the oceans. Connect with that energy now in the Circle of Life.

Likewise acknowledge in a humble way how your own energy somehow marks the space around you so that you yourself can come to dwell in this space at any time. Notice how this space is a unique expression of your own distinct energy, life and purpose in the universe. Breathe deeply and release any tensions remaining in your body.

One simple act of inner growth work is still to be done while still inside your circle. While we have divided the next part of the exercise from this one, the intention was to do the next step now while maintaining your circle. However, if you have a feeling of completion now and want to stop and open another circle in the near future – follow your intuition and trust that your inner being knows what is best for you. When next you open a circle, it will reveal new insights and be a completely new experience. Each time is like this especially during the first years of doing this ceremony. When you are done, close the circle while giving thanks.

Activity 4:3 Reclaiming Personal Space

Open a Circle. As above, tap into the powerful energies of the directions, earth and sky, and when you feel ready, imagine a rather light and not too difficult problem in your daily life that you want to work on. Picture this problem. See it in your mind and hear the sounds you hear during the experience. Feel in your body a bit of what it feels like. Now take this problem from inside your body in a symbolic way. Pull the problem out and into your hands. See the problem for what it looks like when it rests in your hands. What colour is it? What texture does it make? What materials is it made up from? Symbolically place the "problem" in front of you, suspended in mid-air about half an arms breath away. Step back a tiny bit and feel what it feels like to place the problem in its place. Now focus back on the powerful energy of your Sacred Circle. Bring all the power and sense of peace, insight and the feeling of empowerment that you feel in the circle to bear on the smallish problem. Bring all these resources to the problem situation.

At this stage look at the problem in its place. Imagine your arms are now channels of energy that can carry all the power of your Sacred Circle to the problem. Point at the problem in its place. Watch the energy flowing into the problem. Does it look any different now? Wave your strong arm through the air and dispel the problem. It is gone.

Now you can look inward to wherever the problem used to be. Observe how it changed, maybe in some subtle way. Often when we think about emotional and psychic changes it is the smallest change that makes the most difference. It may be that you feel released or the problem just doesn't seem very important anymore. Perhaps nothing changed – in which case you also learned something important. Whatever your experience, say inwardly, 'Thank you inner being, thank you Creator for this insight.'

When you are satisfied that you have experienced these insights enough, take a deep breath and slowly go around the circle to gather up the stones and close the circle. Give thanks for the directions and draw the energy of the circle into your body for healing and renewal. Take up the stones and keep them in a private place for the next time you wish to open a circle to do more inner work.

Joseph Randolph Bowers

5 North: Youth Will See Visions

Northern Door, Grandmother Turtle

Mother of all tribes, nations

Giver of life, Sustainer

Power of Light and Dark

Within your womb, awakening

In the Mi'kmaq Medicine tradition, the North is the place of the tribal Mothers who gave birth and nurture every tribe of humanity. The Grand Mothers are a powerful lot. They come together to determine the needs of the People. Their gathering is a form of Sacred Council. When they Meet, the People sit and listen. Native traditions honour Elder wisdom, and particularly Women's Wisdom, because from the woman's womb all people come forth into this skin-time. Women hold the Power of life and death. They govern the Sacred Worlds because their Medicine is primary and comes before all other forms of knowledge. At the heart of woman's Sacred Medicine are children and youth. This is why we engage the paradox of focusing on youth in this chapter when we could well focus on Elder Medicine given the Sacred Direction of the North. The

Northern Pole in Mi'kmaq cosmology represents the Ancient Origins of All People. In the North rests the Sacred Turtle, upon which the Power of Mother Earth arises. The Earth is formed on the back of the Turtle. It is said that the Thirteen sections on the Turtle Mother's Back came to be when the Creator wished humanity to grow and spread throughout the Earth World. Each quadrant came to be from the Original Grand Mothers who gave birth to the Thirteen Tribes of Humanity.

Today we connect to this Ancient Wisdom because the teachings are still alive and nourish our spirits. It is important to honour Woman's Medicine because both women and men benefit by learning to respect, to care, to nurture and to guide in strong leadership which are all traditional qualities of women in tribal society. At the heart of every Nation are women, children and the elderly. The rest of us exist to take care and serve women, children and the elderly. When a society forgets these ethical and moral standards, that culture begins to break down.

European traditional cultures before the industrial revolution carried these very values. By the time Europeans became colonizers they had all but forgotten their ethical and moral heritage. Today's world bears the burden of this legacy of manipulation, greed, violation, abuse and dominance over creation and other cultures. Getting back to the future of our humanity means we need to regain and reaffirm the Ancient pathways of European tribal origins through various means including the study of Celtic Christian spirituality, Druidic Lore and the Bardic Arts, learning about the Goddess and Matriarchal cultural ways of much of Europe that form our deep origins in culture and identity. How far back do you wish to go? The history is there to explore. And holds much wealth for us today to find our way.

We acknowledge that the mystical path is about practical everyday living while applying these teachings that render life a sacred act based in ethics and moral standards. Remember our definition of mysticism? Mysticism is the practice of spiritual experience. There are many times when intuitions, visions and insights about the bigger picture will break into our awareness. The age of youth and that of elder are the traditional time when visions come to us.

In Women's Medicine the woman's moon time is the traditional time when visions arise. This is when women are at their height of spiritual power and authority. For this reason, in Mi'kmaq culture women tended to seclude themselves during their moon time. Men avoided them at this time, because they were felt to be too spiritually powerful for men to be in their presence.

The spirit of youth is within us. Every developmental stage has a spirit that can be accessed at any time during the lifespan. Although developmental theory has delineated with great precision specific stages of growth from birth to death, life itself is not so clear-cut. Many people do not experience the fullness of any given life stage at the designated time. So, we tend to learn the skills and abilities native to missed steps at some other time. These insights will then need to be integrated into the fullness of being.

Accomplishing these aspects of growth does not need to be a complicated process. However, achieving personal fulfilment does require a degree of commitment and persistence. Visions of the bigger picture of life can take many forms. During youth a blade of grass, a flower or even the patterns found in cement can open doors of awareness to the deeper structure and integrity of life. At other times, a vision of great importance could breakthrough ordinary experience.

This time in human history is another opportunity for people to break out of restrictions. These unsustainable boundaries are created by our busy lifestyles and our incessant priority driven focus on doing actions without a deep abiding conscious awareness. Wisdom has most often been sacrificed for efficiency. Personal presence and relationships usually fall lower and lower on the priority list as the pressures of the day take precedence. These cycles of chronic activity and disembodied energy are perhaps the core addictions of the modern age. Over time people tend to forget the most valuable aspects of life that give us meaning and purpose.

At certain times of the year, we offer token thanks for the value of relationships, but human health cannot rely on such limited offerings. Our beings are crying out for consistent nurturing and care. The human mind, heart and spirit grow through a process of ongoing change and development. Restricting our attentiveness of these important experiences to Christmas, Easter, Thanksgiving and other major holidays is not enough.

It may be a cliché that the spirit of giving that occurs during Christmas ought to exist in our lives every day of the year, but this saying has enormous truth. Bringing the spirit of giving into other days of the year is as simple as a thought that occurs in mind and is followed through by actions centred in love. When we are able to give something of our own that is difficult to give away, we can move beyond the materialistic spirit and enter into the most life-giving part of spiritual giving. There is no specific time of year for this kind of giving.

The spiritual path is often about letting go of attachments and releasing our spirit from the things that bind us. The processes involved are many, but people often ask me how? How do people identify and then release the things that bind and hinder their freedom?

Psychotherapy is in part devoted to answering these questions with practical and therapeutic strategies for quickening the process of healing. All of the spiritual paths that I am aware of in the east and west involve and include processes of unbinding, releasing, transforming and enlightening people to their spiritual potential.

For example, the Christian mystical tradition includes forms of initiation that lead to personal shifts in values and perspective. Originally forms of adult baptism and entering into the body of the church involved an intensive period of retreat from everyday life while learning the stories and traditions of the church. Today the forms of introduction to the culture of faith are focused within a detailed program called the Rite of Christian Initiation of Adults within the western Roman tradition.

Likewise, in the Christian tradition there are strategies used on a daily basis that originally had a purpose of helping people to become free from the things that bind them. For example, the use of holy water for the purification and cleansing the self. While doing so, a person might visualise whatever they have identified that they need to let go of and ask their Higher Power to cleanse them. There are many other methods including the use of smoke, candles, sacred spaces and sanctuaries, holy wells, sacred places of pilgrimage, and other forms of sacramental experiences that are felt to activate spiritual potential.

In Mi'kmaq traditions that I have learned from the Elders there are many ancient and contemporary forms of personal work that help people to heal, to move on, and to be free from the things that bind us. For example, there is an intimate use of sacred smoke from burning of herbs like Sage. White Buffalo Sage for instance is a very fragrant herb that smoulders and produces a beautiful and pungent aroma that sooths the mind and produces a slightly altered state of consciousness. The tradition suggests that the person 'smudge' their aura and body with movements of the hands to bring the smoke over one's body from head to feet. The process is said to unbind our bodies from any unwanted energies or spirits that might attach themselves to us. The person can also visualise whatever they need to let go of and give that back to the Mother to be returned to the earth. Negative emotions and energies from other people can also be cleansed and let go of during this ceremony.

In psychotherapy there is the use of asking people to visualise or write down their burden and place that into a special box the therapist keeps in their office, and then to leave it there and let go of whatever was put inside. These and many other kinds of strategies that people learn over time help them to let go and move on. Indeed, Jesus of Nazareth spoke about giving up our wealth to search for the pearl of great price. Siddhartha the Buddha taught about walking the middle path where detachment nurtures mindfulness. So, allowing the visions of Great Spirit some room to emerge in our minds opens new vistas and breaks open the shutters that guard our eyes. Making this discipline part of an everyday exercise and an attitude of the mind creates pathways in life people otherwise deny themselves. This denial creates discontent.

However, when we open the pathways in our neurology to exploring the realms of creativity and spiritual experience, we open new doorways into mystical experience. The Sacred Circle exercise in the last chapter echoes eons of indigenous wisdom that is revisited in today's context of self-psychology. The principles are the same. When we create sacred space and enter into ceremony, we are using all five sensory systems plus our inner vision and creativity. When we do this, we open parts of our brain normally left un-stimulated. From this ability we create new capacity to discern spiritual experiences when they arise.

It was not without some forethought that the spirit of youth came to be associated with this chapter on visioning. In youth we have capacity for imagination and creative insight that can tend to wane later in life, especially if we give into the pressures of the economy of western values. When we are getting older and wiser, we also need to be regaining our inner youthful vision. This is why the elder in traditional cultures is a person of great power, knowledge and wisdom. Elders are highly respected and never discarded just because they are getting older. Showing elders respect is a sign of a civil society. Elder wisdom suggests that the real test of any spiritual experience is its outcome for the person who experienced that moment in time. The teaching is 'by their fruit you will know them.' What was the outcome? What was changed for the person? How did it benefit them? And here you will often have more meaning revealed than in the actual event itself.

Neither faith nor reason can stand alone. We need both to be whole. Faith is not a blind acceptance of tradition but must be tested and tried by each person. Faith is an approximation of truth that we come to trust over time. We do not always need a depth of feeling or conviction to know something is true. Faith is a realisation that something may hold water. For some people this largely goes without evidence. But faith is not meant to be blind. Psychologically the structure of faith is about a form of reason that comes to believe something is true. Faith builds on reason. But a healthy faith can withstand and will welcome rigorous questioning. We need faith to know that fire is indeed hot; food cooks on a hot stove; and that the sun will actually rise tomorrow. These are all statements of faith and they are for the most part based in a lived 'mystical experience' of reality.

From conscience can arise faith. Many of us go through life only knowing what other people have told us. For whatever reasons we have not taken the journey to discover these spiritual truths ourselves. This kind of faith is no less important and valuable, but of course knowledge handed down is only meant to be a stepping-stone and not the absolute in human growth. We ought to listen to the wisdom of our elders and have respect for the stories that speak of other people's experiences of learning. We can find faith from the stories of other people. Equally, we can be enlightened by written words. But the most sure and strongest form of faith comes from personal experience.

A great Buddhist saying goes: 'If you meet the Buddha, slay him!' This intriguing statement suggests that spiritual awakening comes only from a personal journey. The 'Buddha on the road' that we meet is something or someone external to our path. We need to look inside for enlightenment. Our projections of the Buddha as some external authority or attachment may distract us from our spiritual path.

In our youth we need the strength of elders, the teachings of tradition, and the stability of family to grow strong while holding onto visions of the impossible. At some stage young adults may be given a vision that may seem at first to contradict everything they had learned before. It may take years to unpack. This type of resilience and fortitude can only be learned by example and through longsuffering and endurance. But where are the elders today? Where are the examples of living this life without compromise? Who can youth turn to for an example of being true to the ideals of love, self-sacrifice, responsibility and freedom?

More often than not, there is no one in a youth's everyday life to which they can look up to for mentorship and guidance. Parents and teachers are great for many things, but they are not enough. Every youth needs mentorship, support and encouragement from other sources. Western societies ought to continue considering how to build stronger networks of social support, how to rebuild extended family systems and how to continually highlight the examples of adults who live strong ideals of humanitarianism, spiritual insight and self-sacrifice.

People at any age often need to explore the spirit of youth to regain a sense of vibrancy and engagement with life. Many people come into counselling looking for a deeper connection to the youthful self and to their inner child. Although this has become a great cliché the truth is that within society our focus on work and accomplishment overshadows the more intuitive and spontaneous directions that come from the spirit of childhood and youthfulness. It is another kind of work, a very valuable type of self-development, to give ourselves the space and time we need to explore and nurture the spirit of youth in our lives.

When clients come forward seeking to relive their youth, we often tell them that what they really need is to reconnect with the spirit of youth in their lives today. Their need is not about regaining something from the past. The nostalgia that we feel towards our childhoods is often misplaced. If we take the time to look more deeply, we will see that the lessons we learned during our childhood were valuable and important for that time and place. What we need to learn now as adults is to take on new skill and insight from our inner child that will meet the need of the present moment.

This psychological process is inherently creative and nurturing. The spirit of youth is manifested in our daily lives through giving ourselves space and time to be creative. If we blindly continue the cycle of overwork and chronic stress quite often our bodies will create a crisis that forces us to change our direction. Our nervous system and our physiology require a balance of bodily environmental factors that guard against illness, disease and decay. Obviously, these include good nutrition, consistent sleep patterns, exercise and positive activities along with a meaningful work life. How can people find space to explore the spirit of youth?

Getting in touch with our youthful spirit, we are able to explore the deeper values of humanity. The creative spirit opens us up to engaging in playful and meaningful activities that increase our feeling of being in touch with the world around us. We become empowered to let go of some of our adult conditioning. Indeed, human development and learning happens best when people are relaxed and can enjoy life. One of the best contexts to allow ourselves to let go and become like children again is during vacations, times away and retreats.

As a retreat director we have seen many people enter programs feeling confused, overwhelmed and exhausted in their daily lives. During the retreat they go through several phases. These include initial excitement to the new environment, feeling the need for rest, and then opening the self to new insight and awareness. Soon enough they draw closure to the retreat experience and to re-engage with the world. We are a strong advocate of the retreat experience.

Retreating need not be an expensive endeavour. When making a retreat, we symbolically change the home environment to create a space that is different. This renews an awareness that the impossible may be possible and it shifts the everyday energies of the space to allow for an alternative experience. If we cannot find personal space because of friends or family being around, we will talk to them about the need for space and ask them for a time that is OK when they can do other things. This is a perfect opportunity for a single parent to encourage the function of 'extended families' by asking friends to mind the children for a few hours. Parents can swap baby-sitting times to allow both partners an experience of time away for spiritual reflection.

One lesson people learn as they honour these steps of the path is that we do not need to justify our need for space. We are human beings and part of being a living, breathing and feeling being is the need for downtime. Downtime is not just about sleep, rest and physical recovery. The mind also needs fallow time to ponder the deeper issues of life in a gentle and open-ended way. We do not actually need answers. We already have too much information in the world to deal with. What all of us need is to learn how to live in the questions themselves. We need to learn to breathe. To be quiet and to rest. We need solitude and peace.

Do not be too pushy with your spouse, partner or friends when it comes to sharing your need for space. Expect them to react in different and unpredictable ways. If you are in any way used to being together most of the time it will feel somewhat uncomfortable to ask for space on your own. Though some people may react defensively, underneath they may wonder why you are asking for time alone. This may raise issues of insecurity in your partner or friends. If taking time out to retreat is a very different behaviour than anything you have done before you will in effect be asking for a renegotiation of boundaries around how each of you spend your time alone and together.

While you may be focused on meeting your need for time alone, also be aware that taking this time can best be accomplished with the support of your loved ones. Consider how you can encourage your loved ones and your friends to understand this need, especially if it appears to them something quite different than anything you have asked for in past. I've seen many people react negatively and think taking time alone is very selfish. It is hard not to react to this with defensiveness. But just remember that the people who hold this belief have imposed the same belief on themselves. They do not allow themselves the basic human right for time alone and they most likely see this as a luxury.

Likewise, others may take the request for time alone as extremely threatening. They may think something is wrong with the relationship if you need time away. While this can cause a difficult situation in a relationship, over time the other partner tended to realise that they did not need to feel threatened. In fact, the time they had with the children or alone while the other went on retreat tended to be extremely positive. The other part is growing in trust that when the partner on retreat comes home, they are happy to return and have positive things to share in the relationship from being rested and more at peace.

For many women, realising that they can in fact meet their own needs within the context of their relationships and family life is quite empowering. Likewise, men experience that taking time away from the pressures of their work and family life relieves enormous stress and gives them time to explore their values. Rather than attempting to steal time away while remaining stressed a prearranged retreat provides everyone in the family a positive opportunity to do something different. Instead of taking time away from life and work a well-placed retreat can dramatically increase reserves of energy, resilience and the clarity with which we decide what is important in everyday life.

For most of us adults, taking time away is about the only space we can find to engage with the spirit of youthfulness. Family vacations are a great time for this. But going on a short retreat alone is another way to engage the traditional energy of the vision quest of native cultures. Part of the reason this process is indigenous to youth rests with the fact that during youth people have not yet engaged in adult commitments, relationships, marriage and vocational paths.

Retreating for adults is a way to continue the process of self-exploration and growth. There are few other activities that actually accomplish these goals as well as retreats. If we are like most of our peers, being an adult holds so many demands. The only time we have space in life tends to be much later, in our older age, when we have too much time on our hands and not enough energy or resources to open new pathways. However, by taking these teachings to heart and giving ourselves time to learn through the retreat process, by the time we are older we may also be a bit wiser. Additionally, the time alone that most people face later in life might not be as fearful or difficult provided we have learned how to enjoy our own company through retreat experiences over the years.

You might wonder why a quiet and/or nature-based retreat has anything to do with youth, especially if your own upbringing was busy and active. If you have been thinking this way, consider as an adult how your own children have quality time to engage in play, reading, watching movies, and enjoying the natural environment outside. Young adults might seem very busy, but their orientation to life is open and able to adapt well because they have space and time to learn from each moment. At the heart of this inner psychological ability is the central human capacity for learning, exploring and opening the inner spirit to new awareness. The other way retreats suggest the spirit of youth lies with how youth are presented problems and find solutions. Through the retreat experience we give ourselves time to observe, listen and ponder the contexts of our lives. From this we can find new pathways forward.

Activity 5 Personal Retreat as Self-care

In your journal make an estimate of how much time you spend during each of the following activities. Be specific and calculate the number of hours spent on each activity. This process is a way of evaluating and examining how you invest your energy. This best estimate will assist you as you begin to plan how you can take time out for a personal retreat. The activities that make up most of your time may or may not be included in the following categories:

- Work
- Minding the children
- Preparing meals
- Studying
- Fixing, doing chores, tending the property
- Travel to work and home or for business
- Vacation time
- Quiet time, prayer, church or spiritual ritual
- Doing a hobby; crocheting, fixing the car, painting…
- Any other activity

After you have written down the hours for each of the above and examined how you spend your time, ask yourself how much time would you like to devote to a retreat experience? Over the long term, if you were to build in a regular routine of taking a retreat one or two times a year or every two or three months, how much time could you give to doing this?

Retreats can be any length of time. They can go from two or three hours to two or three days or longer. The length of time does not necessarily equate with the effectiveness and rewards gained from a retreat. Often times shorter retreats are more valuable if they are done regularly. It is also recommended to take shorter retreats initially and build up over time towards taking a longer retreat that goes two or three days. Knowing this, make a realistic plan of how you will take the time out that you need for a retreat.

Consider if you can take a retreat at a bed and breakfast or to a church run retreat centre, a health centre or spa or any other retreat place. National parks often have cabins to rent for a few days. Caravan and camping parks tend to be inexpensive and quite fun to visit. Stretch your realm of possibilities. Sometimes people may take a day off when traveling for work and might go for a hike in a national park or rent a luxury suite in a hotel with a spa bath and swimming pool. Sometimes retreats are alone or with friends and family. Other times they are more structured with a retreat director or spiritual guide.

Clients in counselling have often travelled across country and rented a motel room in a quiet place and had longer sessions over a three-day weekend. This provided either an individual or a couple time away that combined a retreat experience with counselling psychotherapy. There are many options out there when you begin to explore them. We have found that the depth of client's work increases and becomes quite transformative when they take a two- or three-day weekend to focus on personal work in therapy. Not only do they engage the sessions with me, which usually occur during morning and afternoon hours, but they also have time alone or in doing physical activities or even enjoying a bit of retail therapy. This provides them with reflective space and time to relax during the often-challenging work of personal change making.

Remember to consider how you will share this information with your partner and friends. While researching your options invite and include your family and friends in your planning process. Encourage them to imagine taking time out for themselves in the future.

Give yourself and your family time after the retreat to talk, to re-engage and to share the insights and experiences of the time apart. It helps enormously to plan this time well. For example, by getting home in the early afternoon on Sunday plan to spend the afternoon with your partner and family sharing a picnic or time in the garden. This may be better than arriving home late and having to start work the next day. This also provides your family time to settle their minds. Remember they too have had a different experience and may have many thoughts and perhaps also apprehensions about the underlying reasons for your taking time away. Naturally, they like you will have had many ideas, thoughts and feelings over the weekend that could be shared at some stage. Give things time. Allow for expressions of love, caring and concern. And try to stay open minded and supportive when your family may not understand your need for space.

A retreat experience can help to build up strength and respectfulness in relationships when well planned. Having time alone is another form of building positive boundaries and realising in new ways that you can choose when to allow people into your space and when to draw back a bit to find your own way.

One of the oldest indigenous models of retreats found in many tribes around the world and echoed in western mystical traditions, is that one person takes over the chores of the day while the other person takes the place of rest and retreat. Usually a third person helps with things like cooking and tending the needs of the person on retreat while keeping watch. If you think creatively about this three-person model you may be able to accomplish this with a friend and your partner or with another couple. Write your thoughts and ideas in your journal and enjoy planning your retreat experiences. We wish you every peace and blessing.

Joseph Randolph Bowers

6 Above: Personal Transformation

Sky world above, stars of night

Honour, dancing, ceremony, take flight

Ancestors, Saints, Custodians

Powers of Life, Creator

Paths of enlightenment, paths of darkness

When a seed falls to the ground it undergoes a symbolic death. It may lie dormant through winter months and then in spring its husk will suddenly crack open. Moisture works its magic and the seed is transformed into a shoot of new growth. From this shoot branches out many arms and hands reaching toward the sun. Tiny roots dip into the soil and begin establishing a base for nurturing and sustaining life. In many ways our lives are like the seed, the husk, the spout, the roots and the branches.

Each and every development of the seed requires an environment that is conducive to new growth, to a fundamental and transformational change. Likewise, every human development has a context in which the change is created and sustained. Sometimes life seems to burst forth with spontaneous growth. At such times, the emergence of new developments can seem out of place and inappropriate. The system, the ecology or the human mind and heart are not prepared for the change that occurs. At such times personal transformation can become a crisis.

When a spiritual emergency happens, most people have no framework to understand. For example, when a 'psychic insight' breaks into awareness, such as a precognition of future events, people do not know what to do. Many suspect mental illness. The fear of being labelled crazy causes much stress. The social context we live in does not typically support these experiences and because our social isolation includes a lack of role models, no elders or people who have travelled the road before us are near to offer assistance.

In my estimation we have forgotten who we are. Modern society does not offer us a context for understanding human consciousness. There is no road map for being human and no manual for gaining and guiding spiritual insight. Indigenous cultures around the world have strong cultural contexts for understanding and processing these natural insights. Rituals of initiation, healing and recognition of social roles for people who are gifted in intuitive ways are supported by the indigenous community. Skills of intuition, spiritual insight and healing are not felt to be exceptional and are an accepted part of people's roles in the social network. Role models and mentors are made available to the community should anyone need help in these important areas of human growth, potential and challenge.

The spiritual path is not easy. Ironically, the last thing we wish to do is encourage people to take up the spiritual path because it inevitably involves self-sacrifice and includes levels of awareness that often causes suffering. The closer we are to the truth of Life, the more difficult it can be to live in our conflicted modern world. Likewise, with the inspiration of Spirit we are able to take on the roles of responsibility and care for the human family and to bear the burdens of our awareness with a degree of grace and peace of mind.

On one hand, spirituality is a more general field of making meaning from life events. Spirituality is also about generating inner hope, resilience and fortitude in the face of difficult life events. On the other hand, psychic level phenomena appear to cut across what we consider to be normal human capacities for insight and awareness. At some juncture the more general arena of spirituality crosses into unexplained physical and psychological phenomena. These frontiers hold many fascinating challenges for science to explore.

Within many traditional Indigenous cultures, a philosophy of interconnection supports the notion that people's senses are not limited by only five physical sensory systems that must only observe what is right in front of one's nose. Native spirituality and culture work in an interconnected mystical universe that is intimate and close to each person. This world is not so distant and is not distinct and separate. We can feel the connections across time and space. We can through vision and inner knowing experience great detail without actually physically being present in the same place.

Native perspectives also include awareness of other plant and animal life as part of our personal family relations. All things are our brothers and sisters. Our Ancestors live in river stones. Our parents and siblings who have passed on may exist in the spirit of animals that come into our lives. And through processes of vision and questing we can experience what it is like to run with the wolves, fly with the eagles and swim in the depths of the ocean with the whales. These experiences suggest that our senses can come to include the sensory worlds of other animals.

Obviously how we view our senses relies heavily on culture and values. When people have a cultural and value-based context to experience spiritual phenomena, they may have a greater capacity for spiritual experience. When a culture changes and denies that these things can happen, and then forms philosophies and beliefs that do not allow for spiritual and intuitive abilities, it appears that less people experience spiritual phenomena. Because human beings are cybernetic dynamic and holistic creatures, by limiting their outlook to such an extreme people tend to fall into a crisis of meaning. Instead of opening up new insight, materialistic philosophies close off possibilities. Spiritual forms of knowledge are cast as left-wing psychic phenomena and are discounted.

However, life has many ways to open knowledge to us. We ought to realise that what the west considers the 'five senses' is a rather limiting view of human capacity. There is hope for humanity because the human spirit has shown again and again in countless way that we are more than what we feel, more than what we think. Evolutionary history shows that people have incredible creative and problem-solving power to change their circumstances. People can alter the course of events that lie ahead by pure will power, and through exercising love, care and concern for other's wellbeing. How is this any different from what we classify as psychic phenomena? In fact, we are looking at a spectrum of capacities that all people possess.

From this, it makes more sense that healing is possible and does happen. These realities manifest in blunt physical ways and in subtle and immaterial ways. For example, most people will admit that the presence of another person influences their interactions with others. If we can change so easily based on only the presence of one person, how much more can be experience within ourselves?

Another thought-provoking insight is regarding the nature of faith. Faith may be the substance of things unseen by the plain eye of observation, but faith is also a certainty of awareness that can be observed through more subtle sensory and intuitive insight. Healing is possible because of observing the process of healing in people's lives. Healing happens at physical, emotional, psychological and spiritual levels. From the eye of well-balanced 'faith' within counselling psychotherapy we observe that people's deepest inclination is toward healing and wholeness.

This led to looking more closely at the processes of change and evolution. Though Darwin suggested that natural selection was at work in evolutionary change the theory itself warrants the acknowledgement of a kind of natural wisdom inherent in creation. In more recent times the theory has been challenged because evolution is far messier and more unpredictable than Darwin allowed. Nonetheless, ecosystems and species appear to undergo changes that incorporate phases of growth, disintegration, death, regeneration and reintegration. These cycles or spirals of evolution parallel human physical and psychic change at micro and macro levels.

Ironically Darwin's enduring message was not that the strongest species survive, but that the species most able to adapt and change will be the ones to flourish over all others. There is a deeply spiritual message hidden within the very theory of western scientific evolutionism. We need to remain open of mind and heart, and able to adapt and change as needed. Indeed, the defining mark of humanity is our innate ability to predict and foreshadow adaptive changes that enable us to face the challenges that lie ahead.

Looking at these phenomena it is logical to wonder from where does creation get such intricate patterns of change? It is possible that there is no wisdom guiding evolutionary events. It is equally possible that Life has its own supra-codes of intelligence, much like our bodies hold encoded DNA, and that a body of knowledge lies outside of human everyday awareness and awaits discovery. Science is constantly pushing the boundaries of the known universe.

It is not inconceivable that science will one day prove the existence of a Higher Power, a Creator if you will, even though I reckon this has already been accomplished in the way that I understand divinity as a part of the life force of all things that exist. In many ways, looking at the evidence compiled thus far it is a reasonable conclusion that Life is inherently intelligent.

For these reasons it seems that personal transformation is the desire of Life for everyone. Human beings are encoded with abilities and desires that suggest the Creator's own personal touch in our make-up. Our place in the order of nature warrants the notion that we are on the path of transformation from unsustainable consciousness to a deep abiding connection with Life. Our destination is not otherworldly.

For example, we have wondered what the expectation of the second coming of Jesus really means. In more contemplative moments we have come to understand that the second coming is a metaphor for human transformation. Jesus comes to us for the second time 'at the end of the eon' when we change our awareness enough to once again be at one with Creation, the universe, and our Creator. The second coming of Jesus is a story that describes the evolution of human consciousness. The physical reality of Jesus coming on the clouds may or may not happen in the future and this belief relies more heavily on faith. But in the minimum the story suggests that human beings can and do change.

People have asked me what would the world be like if we all found spiritual enlightenment? My reply is we have enough worries for today. Let's worry about that future situation when we all get there together, OK?

Our lives will always present many challenges, as this is part of human life. Living in greater balance, peace and spiritual awareness can only increase our enjoyment and happiness in life. Our bodies, nervous systems, organs and our minds will be more receptive to beauty and less conditioned to accept suffering and war.

There will never likely be a utopia where sickness and death are eliminated. The nature of our psychic evolution and developmental cycles warrant times of upheaval and disquiet. How we come to respond to these challenges determines our degree of maturity and wisdom.

When we come back into balance and find our energy united with the earth and at one with the sky our dreams begin to come true. It has been said that long before white men came to First Nations lands Elders of great insight had visions. They saw the arrival of the white men. Some saw the devastation that resulted and the exploitation of Mother Earth. Many could see no further as the psychic weight of these visions was too great.

Others with older wisdom in their spirits saw a time when Mother Earth would cleanse herself of the harm and disease inflicted by the white man. One prophecy foretold a time when red hearts would be born in white bodies and white hearts would be born in red bodies. During those times at the end of the world human beings would be given channels to insight and awareness that might address the imbalances created over many generations. Our circumstances today are in relationship to all events and situations that came before now. How we respond is up to us and will no doubt effect the next seven generations.

Heaven is where dreams come true. Heaven as a place outside of the world of life on earth? I've not been there except in the body and in the mindfulness of prayer. Such a place may exist. But we will not know this in experience until something brings us there in fullness.

Then we may look back and have a grand old laugh at past ignorance. Our beliefs for today are tested and tried and are from this place. Here and now. Heaven is where we belong. Heaven is here and now.

Heaven is a place where we grow to find fulfilment, love and peace in our hearts. This can be anywhere and perhaps it is true that our lives merely go through another personal transformation when we leave our bodies. It is good to have our western beliefs challenged and to know that we can honour and respect aboriginal cultural views and values that provide a more open and accommodating space to explore spiritual experiences.

Regardless what beliefs we hold, the crisis of change that people face at various turns are all about making sense of the contingencies of life, illness, death and how to find happiness. We are all trying to make sense of life that really makes no sense, because it is too complicated and too interwoven for us to really embrace in fullness.

You may seek money, power, influence, control, work, play, pleasure, relationships or solitude. Whatever you desire in life we can guarantee the core desire of your deepest longings is to be happy, to find some peace of heart.

Your motivation in life may be humanitarian or environmental. But at the core you seek to be happy in creation and to see that other creatures share in your joy and freedom.

What a profound realisation it is to awaken to the reality that we can have this now. While we work for the liberation of others, we can experience what we seek in the now. Indeed, one of the greatest secrets of manifesting the awakening of humanity is that the most important thing we can do is to open our inner world, become centred and grounded, and grow into enlightenment right here and now.

Reality is, what you seek is only a thought and a decision away. We do not need a drug or a party or food to fill the hole inside our hearts. All we need is to breathe deeply, take in the air and energy of life and to access the part of our spirits that are infinitely powerful. When we find this place of inner calm, we realise that it always existed within us. It takes but a little bit of discipline and practice to access this place of contentment.

We are all in ways like Humpty Dumpty. We fall off the wall of life and get very confused and upset by things that distract us from who we really are. We take enormous expense and effort to find ourselves again. Counselling, medicine, travel, pilgrimage, church, books, television, education… we look in so many areas to find a simple truth… the meaning of life…

We are all looking for the meaning of life. But the secret of life is that we make meaning after experiencing anything. Meaning cannot be constructed apart from lived experience.

What people seek most is an experience of love, peace, being understood, being heard. People crave the sort of knowledge we describe here when life itself breaks into our awareness and then we know. We are absolutely certain. No one can take away our own experience.

At this point some people will intellectually move to constructivism, claiming that my approach is about personal meaning creation – that the meaning in life is whatever people place on their experiences. In one sense this is true. In another sense meaning is not so trivial. We do not of ourselves have the power or presumption to define meaning in life. Rather we are only one part of the process.

Meaning is both deductive (given to us by Life and through intellectual and cognitive awakening) and inductive (arising within us through direct experience and learning). Western constructivism however posits that people make meaning out of experience, as if meaning is something material that people make like a skateboard or iPhone. Constructivism in this sense is a form of western materialism that denies the wider and holistic origins of meaning and insight within creation, in ecological relations, and in wider social, cultural and spiritual traditions.

In contrast, allow me to pause and share my philosophy of life. My approach celebrates the idealism of Hegel (1770-1831) who suggested that there is a pre-existing nature of reality within creation. We cannot construct such a reality because it exists apart from us, has its own integrity and power. We can indeed participate and form relationships with this wisdom and knowledge. Hegel also taught about the 'the mind of the creator' as an origin of knowledge and power that we can discern within creation and perhaps directly through mystical experience and by growing in knowledge.

These origins of meaning outside of us form important parts of our own meaning making through observation of spiritual and ecological phenomena, and by forming balanced relationships within the ecology. While we acknowledge that a personal approach to life is grounded in spirituality and faith as processes of learning, these are also informed and challenged by reason.

Combined with this approach, human beings possess a something like a soul; and we would side with Plato's (427-337 BCE) foundational aesthetics of identity. He based human identity within a spiritual entity inhabiting a material body. This notion was picked up throughout the history of psychology and is the basis of the term 'psychotherapist' which means, a 'doctor or healer of the soul.'

Within this philosophy is a respect for the history of western and eastern mysticism, theology, Christian teachings, and a deep abiding respect for eastern wisdom traditions such as Buddhism. The approach integrates well with Native North American and Aboriginal Australian traditions, as well as many other indigenous cultural ways. At the core, in humility and respect, the world is steeped in mystery, wonder, the unknown and unknowable. This spirituality allows for continual growth in awareness arising from the Great Oneness, which existed long before me and will continue long after we are gone from the physical body.

Likewise, the practice of learning and awakening is guided by an instinctual scholastic sensibility that stands with great minds like St Bonaventure, St Francis of Assisi, and St Thomas Aquinas. These scholars and mystics taught about the interconnection of all life, and that we find meaning and God when we enter into relationship with the creation. God is not far off for us human souls, because we find God through the creation.

Kin with this early exposure to the classical methods of western Christianity are the Indigenous methods based in respect for tribal cosmologies. These maps of reality and the cosmos provide incredible insight into the mystery of how life and all of creation are interconnected. Aboriginal ways honour the knowledge based in local ecologies, and the ancient wisdom traditions that are handed down from the Elders over tens of thousands of years.

These teachings form cultural and spiritual practices in ceremony, education, economy, trade, as well as within change, development, and in life. From these deep spiritual roots arise the interconnected circles and spirals that represent my philosophy of life, my teaching, scholarship and practice.

Earlier in this book we mentioned how the various parts of life can form an integrated synthesis, and this circle or cluster of meanings is a more exact and illustrative example of putting together a picture of meaning that forms a philosophy of life and practice. This task has taken the better part of thirty years, so cannot be rushed nor imposed from external forces.

Many elements are included in this circular spiral map of reality. On one side of life we have learned the deconstructive critical analytical tools of the western academe. These are steeped in materialism and constructivism. Even though we do not include these philosophies as an integral part of identity, they are expressed in work quite often. Thus, these are merely tools. They cause enormous existential anxiety for many people as they seek to deconstruct the world without respect, a world that intuitively we know to be real and true.

And yet, we suspect many compatriots engage in a material philosophy without much regard for other forms of belief and value, while assuming that a constructivist map of reality is correct and without need for further questioning. Indeed, if this be true, it would be much better to live within the paradox of doubt and questioning, which is due to the conscious choice to live within a more complex phenomenal world that includes layers of reality that constructivism and western materialism cannot imagine nor abide.

This being said, your philosophy and practice can be based in a Hegelian acknowledgement of exploration, discovery and questioning as the basis of growth and awareness. You can embrace paradox as essential to faith and reason. Your embodiment helps to define your approach, as any philosophy worth its space and time ought to be incarnated within flesh and bone. This is not a form of existentialism or of humanism, which suggest that phenomenal reality can be observed and reproduced by what is seen and heard without direct acknowledgement that part of the reality we experience exists as part of the creation prior to our conscious awareness.

Likewise, the tension arises because much of western theory and practice across the helping professions is based in humanism and existentialism, which give rise to methods of phenomenology and critical social theory as tools used to great effect in academic work. These inspire traditions of grounded theory, ethnography, and autobiography, which are also based in cultural frames of reference. These approaches are steeped in empiricism and materialism and have been important methods during parts of our collective scholarly life.

But just as much as these approaches and the underlying values they suggest are useful, they are equally problematic. Adding to this, they often remain hidden from people's awareness in the everyday exercise of education and training across the professions.

When subjected to critical analysis, itself a tool encouraged by the proponents of these theories, as well as standpoint theories based in alternative non-western perspectives, we find that the mainstream methods of western social science are themselves quite disturbing. We uncover deeply biased, prejudiced, colonial, gender-based and racist assumptions that have guided these methods throughout western history and that have only gone underground recently due to political correctness. But when we read the sources, we find these issues, take a pause, and then question the assumptions that underpin whole disciplines like psychology, psychotherapy, counselling, nursing, social work and medicine.

The approach then seeks to de-centre the modern era by acknowledging a wider grounding culturally and historically. For example, we appreciate and celebrate the purity of the Franciscan and Dominican medieval traditions that influenced youth. At the same time, we find a huge amount of wisdom comes to me from Indigenous traditions. These hold many keys to the long-term sustainability of theory and practice within mainstream western cultures. Western methods can only be entertained with a great deal of postmodern and postcolonial critique that seeks to deflate the claims of philosophies like humanism, and to slowly break open the cosmic egg of western theory that has sustained and perpetuated dominant approaches across the professions.

After reflecting on the place of each philosophy as we get older and live life instead of make theory, our path affirms the experiential, poetic, theistic, spiritual, marginal, metaphorical, and numinous.

After much testing and trials, we find we are coming back to the basic beliefs that inspired us to take up professional life in the first place. These are beliefs and values based in faith, hope, and love. These are a sense of calling in life that is planted in a basic feeling for the goodness of offering our life in service to others as a spiritual gifting. It is tempting to agree with St Francis of Assisi when he said that intellectual life is a distraction to the spirit, and a temptation of ego. It was not without significance that we received the name Francis from homeless man on the streets of Halifax during youth, and more formally during 2006, when our sacred spiritual vows were affirmed by fellow Franciscans in Australia.

In this way, part of past challenges of academic life demanded that we put aside a service-based orientation and engage in research and writing that expressed another form of value not kin to the spirit. This deadlock needed to change, diffuse, and become more balanced; and more in-tune with basic approaches to life. In that way we needed to cleanse and let go of many things that clouded what Creator was trying to communicate as of purpose and meaning in life. Afterall, our life is about speaking with Spirit, writing from the heart, and helping others. This meant that when lost, we had to get back on the path again. We each need to find our way through many challenges and the process can take several years.

This being said, as we honour a core sensibility the other tools find their place. The more strength in who you are within yourself, the less the power of others to push you around and make you feel inadequate. Just because some people think of their views as 'contemporary' does not mean those perspectives are of greater value or validity.

Indeed, when you test your views over time you may come to feel that your philosophy is well balanced and provides room for critique and change. The very thought that one's beliefs would be judged in any way by others is foreign. There is room for everyone and the greater the diversity in creation the more we have to learn from each other. Yet this resistance and push from others to conform to their worldviews teaches us much about life. In the long run this can help you to come to terms with your own way.

People are esteemed equals. We are spiritual entities worthy of profound respect. We are spirits who are on their own vision quest while seeking their way through life. Our task is to help others find the next few steps on their path. Not to tell them what to do! Not to influence them! And not to suggest to them that this way or that way might be better! Rather, our purpose is to offer others reassurance that they can find for themselves the next steps in life, and then to stand beside them while they make their own choices.

We have often become an advocate for others within the constraints of institutions that tend to forget why they exist. All institutions exist to serve people, not the other way around. Rules and policies are meant to be written by informed minds that can also interpret and bend interpretations to help others when they need help.

Our purpose is to open the wealth of other people's minds and hearts by pointing to what already exists within them. They only need to explore their own creativity and power. We can help them open up and activate their innate human and spiritual potential. These are some of my fondest values when working with people across the professions and as a teacher, lecturer, writer and mystic.

For those with the certainty of faith there is a loving Presence in the universe. There is a path to walk that gives us purpose. We really do stand on the threshold of becoming divine beings. Our evolutionary path is towards ever more subtle expressions of consciousness that draw us back to where we already are. The second coming of Jesus, the enlightenment promised by Buddha, the path described by Mohammad, these transformations are happening now in people's everyday lives. And however heavenly our insights we will always come back to the basics of improving the physical conditions of life on this planet. This is the greatest challenge we can ever face and the most rewarding, indeed.

Spirituality is at the root extremely practical and what we need most on earth is clean water and for people to have enough food to eat. We need to stop polluting the environment and destroying forests, lakes and rivers. Even the great oceans of the world are becoming choked by pollution. These are the concerns of our lives that need to be addressed. They impact everything we do and cut to the core of our identity. No greater challenge awaits this generation.

But if having spiritual insights, intuitive visions or a feeling of connection to life is necessary for people to become mobilised to respond to the crisis humanity now faces, then by all means, this book is dedicated to opening these doors. Once you grasp the whole, the parts make more sense. Spiritual experiences and mystical awareness open up the senses to new awareness of what life really means – and central to this is that we are not alone, we do not exist in separate boxes and our lives are intimately connected with each other and the environments within the planetary system.

Faith may also assist us in confronting the demons of our demise. Faith is not a useless experience. The nature of faith is built into the fabric of human consciousness. Inside faith is the ability to know something and then trust what you know is true. Faith is sister to Doubt and these two powers work together to help us navigate the billions of insights, thoughts and questions that flow through us like electrical currents from the time of our conception to the time of our body expiring. The delicate balance of life relies on faith to give our beings just enough balance to continue without falling over.

We must remember also that if people are out of balance, then people can redirect their actions to bring balance back into place. If earth ecosystems have been destroyed, they may never be the same again. But all ecosystems contain the energy of life and as such have the ability to heal over time. We must never lose hope. The Spirit of Life is that power and energy within all living and non-living beings and when we work in alignment with the Spirit of Life, we may find ways to assist in widespread regeneration of our environment.

Nature dreams her own balance through storms and quiet. She knows when all things are in conflict and at peace. If you have ever walked through the untouched forests of Canada, you will understand this truth. The pressing issues we face can be addressed even if social revolution becomes necessary to change the mechanisms of power that support polluting the environment. Each of us plays a part. One drop can raise the sea. This is not the place for me to suggest what your role should be. You must look around your own world and find a way to act that is best for you, for your circumstances, and for the lives of the people and other beings in your world. But as much as you may seek spiritual insight, remember that you must eat, feed the body and that you are in relationship with the earth where your food comes from. We are not disembodied spirits.

There are always more thresholds to explore. Each place holds its own wisdom, strength and surety. We can rely on the ecology and the Ancient Spirits of Place to guide us in life. This does not refer to some otherworldly teaching. Rather, Aboriginal wisdom knows that our Ancestors are all around us and have become part of the essence of the landscape. Not only this, but the energy of the cosmos is available to us when we respect the ecology around us – the source of the very process of evolution is accessible in each rock, hill, tree, stone – in all things that exist.

Remember that like there are boundaries and laws of culture there are also spiritual territories and laws of being. One law that is rarely challenged is the sacredness of personal space, particularly space that is dedicated to spiritual ritual. Energies cannot enter personal ritual space that is dedicated to healing and spiritual growth unless those energies are invited. Claim your space, your energetic field as your own. This is as simple to do as the thought.

By claiming your space, you are empowering your body-mind and your spirit to occupy your space in the cosmos. You are taking the first steps in the process of cleansing your being of unwelcome spirits that come to attach themselves to us over time. These spirits are the energetic systems of other people whose agendas and fears enter our being in subtle ways. Some energy of others wants to dominate us. Others want to control, influence or guide us. Other spirits seek to nurture us in freedom. Many of these energies we seek out and they are positive for our development, like the energy of a teacher or mentor.

Other energies are harmful and cause us to doubt our self-worth, identity and directions in life. Shadow emotions create many subtle energetic systems that can come to dominate our lives over time until some crisis forces us to realise how far we have changed for the worse. For example, addictions to substances, gambling, food and over-work can often be traced to the unconscious acceptance of energetic systems of thought and action that defeat our primary self-worth. These energies deny our core identity as children of Creation and set us on a path of self-destruction.

Certain energies want to take from us. There are many people who take and do not give back. They have not learned the path of love, only the way of receiving energy for survival. These people cannot abide with themselves for even a moment.

They need the constant stimulation of other people and events around them to sustain their lack of identity. There are other people who live life not knowing how to give or receive. They fumble through their days, making constant mistakes of judgment. And there are many more people who know how to give but they cannot allow themselves to receive. The impulse to always give sustains a deeper fear of becoming vulnerable to receiving the energy of love from others.

People who always give and do not give others the opportunity to give to them live a sort of reverse-psychology of selfishness. Everyone may see these people as self-less and spiritual. But in reality, constant giving depletes their spirits and underneath a martyr complex is nurtured. In this deeper place these people feel short-shifted, let down and very lonely. By not learning, they are unable to receive; and this leaves them isolated, alienated, and unfulfilled. Opening up to receiving is just as difficult a lesson for these people as it is hard for a taker to learn to give. But both extremes come from the same place.

Be a gift… and receive the gift of others. Be strong and be vulnerable. Take care and be taken care of.

Jesus of Nazareth said that in our weakness is our strength. When we are weak, when our fears dominate us and when the energies of shadow spirits overwhelm our lives in conflicting emotions this is when we have the greatest opportunity to experience the realisation that we are children of light. This is when we can say in an instant, enough! And in our mind and heart the storms of our being can be dispelled. We have more to learn from our weaknesses than from any other personal data and most often our greatest strength grows out of our greatest weakness.

Likewise, when we believe we are strongest we are at our weakest. The path of humility is always surer than building ourselves up to be the best. Surely, we empower ourselves to believe that we can be the best! But it is not a place of psychic security to assume we are strong when we are in fact always very human.

Buddhist wisdom suggests taking the middle road between extremes. To be neither strong, nor weak and to find our way by attending to our actions in the spirit of compassion, this is to find freedom. In the Christian sense this is to live the gospel message. In counselling psychotherapy terms this is to nurture mental health and wellness.

Our beings are inherently spiritual, that is, we are structured to sustain growth and change. We are beings that evolve. Basic cognitive insight builds with emotional intelligence and these together sustain psychological insight. Relational experiences contribute to our identity and our beings expand to take on more depth. At some point in our development subtle level insights may emerge and the basic systems that govern our lives take on new meaning. Awareness expands and psychic insight and experiences add to spiritual-level beliefs and values.

These transpersonal levels of being hold the greatest potential to change and transform our lives. Holistic and integrative healing accelerates when we are on our path. This in turn influences our future actions and the world around us. Flexibility, visioning, intuiting and navigating new paths are possible. All our choices at this level take on a deeper significance and spiritual power. We understand now how we are interconnected with all beings. We hold them in esteem and consider how our actions impact on others. We are in relationship with our environment. We are kin within our ecology. No longer do we act in selfish motivation that denies this relational context. We are growing into a global ethic of care and compassion. Our awareness goes beyond time. In this now we are aware of the next seven generations. We know intimately that we are actually one with each and every generation that will come after us in the future.

We are one. What we do to ourselves we do to our children and our children's children. From this place it is not a burden to care for the earth, to give back to our environment. From this place we gladly make concessions for the sake of future generations.

Caring for others is simply doing what is right, what is good and part of our being. Such acts of compassion are a natural manifestation of our divine life, our identity and our path work. These ethics hold the hope for a lasting global peace. This can occur when more people on earth share this understanding. We can work together to create a world where people want to belong.

Activity 6 Intuitive Awakening

This activity follows through on the next steps involved in opening up intuitive insight. We need to understand clearly that personal worlds are tied to global trends. Individual values are linked to cultural ethics. The way we come to manifest our own lives influences the people around us. They in turn influence others. Inner peace leads to a global awakening.

We have only to understand the physics of one stone dropped into the clear waters of a lake. When you picture the ripples expanding outward you realise your inner power is surely just as great. This philosophy of life starts with realising that you are not alone. You are part of everything that exists.

Now regardless what sensory systems you have been exploring, begin to think about someone you love in the world who is not with you physically in the same location. Choose someone you have not seen today so that you do not know what they are wearing or where they are or what they are doing. You may actually want to let the person know you are doing this activity and ask them if you can borrow a watch or bracelet. Take note of the time and day you try this in your journal. If you can, hold an object that this person has worn on their body. Don't try to 'pick up' anything. Just rest into your awareness and breathe, in and out, in and out…

Ask yourself, what are they doing now? As you sense whatever comes up inside you, be aware of where this knowledge comes from in your sensory systems. Jot down your sensations and insights. Try to sense what the person is feeling. How does this sensation come to you? Write out your experience. What colours is the person wearing? Do you see this, feel it or hear it? Taste it or smell it? What pieces of clothing are they wearing? What do they smell like? Are they wearing perfume? What fragrance is it?

Consider if you can discern any other pieces of information about the person in the now. And be aware of which part is most challenging and the parts you cannot do. There may be many reasons why insights do not come forward. Be patient and accepting. Go inward and thank your inner being for assisting you and accept inwardly the inherent wisdom of your being. Another strategy to open intuition is the following.

Get together with a colleague, friend or partner. Sit back to back in two chairs, so that only your shoulders are touching. One person will think of a person in their mind. The other participant will try to sense, see, hear, taste or touch in some way the imagined person. Whatever way at all, the person who is sensing will try to describe the person being thought about. The one who is thinking of someone offers no clues. People often can't control themselves and will offer at least a yes or no kind of response, or a hot or cold comment, which gives the 'intuitive' an idea of whether they are on the right track or not. The person sensing continues to describe the experience in sensory terms, whatever bits and pieces come up, even if they make no sense. When the person has tried their best and feels like they are finished, discuss.

Often students engaging this activity will give up too quickly. Instead, take a pause and breathe deeply. We can only pick up on hidden knowledge when we are in the right frame of mind and heart. We then do a breathing and relaxation exercise and when they are ready to continue, it is much more likely that they may get more from the 'intuitive seeking' than otherwise. Once the partners finish the first run through, reverse roles. The next step after this is that one of the pair thinks of a place that you would love to be. Bring yourself there and feel, see, hear, taste and smell that place to the fullest you can. The other person works to sense the place and to describe it in sensory terms. Discuss and reverse roles.

7 Below: Healing Yourself and Others

Earth world, Under world, Deeps

Pulsing drum of Mother beats

Steady, walking one foot in pace

Attending, listening, learning

Knowledge, humility, respect

Life on earth relies on a fragile balance. All of life is energy. Energy by its nature ebbs and flows, and nothing remains the same. To comprehend problems of health, emotions, psychology, relationships and spiritual difficulties we need to first understand the nature of healing. To understand the concept, we look to the primary processes of life, health, and illness. Wellness and disease arise from changes in energy over time. Balance within a system promotes health. Imbalance and blockage results in illness.

Healing is another form of energetic change. The dynamic is guided by holistic and systemic flows of energy across complex and interacting spheres of influence. Energy is found in everything and moves between everything. The classic example of 'the Force be with you' is inspired by ancient teachings found in the mystical traditions of many religions and indigenous worldviews. Modern physics is rediscovering these age-old teachings through systematic analysis of energetic systems that govern the ecosystem. Likewise, the discoveries of physics suggest that in the process of observing energy and movement we influence that which we observe. All things are in relationship. We are not isolated in our minds and bodies. We actually have a synergetic interaction with everything around us. We have a primary role in our own healing. Healing is also quite relational.

We can never simply observe phenomena and remain distant or cold. But ironically, in our dominant social beliefs we have separated ourselves from each other and from the earth. We shield ourselves from the reality of our profound interdependence. When isolation exists, healing is much more difficult to accomplish. These thoughts that discriminate, set apart and isolate us from each other and the environment might arise from many human illusions like fear, pride, power or desire and may feed selfish outcomes like self-protection, dominance, control and influencing others. But fundamentally these habits of thought are immature and lead to false outcomes. These beliefs do not sustain life. These blockages become embedded in our bodies.

Our alienation from each other generates environments of fear, anxiety, regret, stress and social unrest. These emotive and energetic interactions result in creating stereotypes that justify our thought patterns and increase the likelihood of prejudices that prevent people from breaking out of negative habits. These systems of belief hinder people waking up to signs of crisis. These biased ways of filtering information condition people to limiting views of the world. Many crisis of health come about from these patterns. These shadow human energies appear to cause social disintegration and result in increased overuse of medical and social security systems. The overall cost of negative human thoughts and actions is unfathomable. As Buddha suggested, the endless cycle of human suffering continues while people go about their daily lives, never putting two and two together.

The answers to many of our problems lies between our ears and behind our eyes. All the prophets including Jesus of Nazareth pointed people in the direction of self-awareness. When someone awakens, and realises that all of life is interconnected, the next thought to come is so what? What can I do with this? What does it matter? The answer to these questions depends almost solely on who is asking them. For someone new to these realms many new pathways will open up. To others who are already on the path, the emphasis is not so much on newness as on deepening the journey.

For those who walk this way, the spiritual realms are their native land. Opening in this skin-time to new awakening may lead old souls to realise how flawed today's world really has become. This leads us to profound compassion. Modern societies are lost in a maze of confusion. From a spiritual place old souls can feel quite depressed while carrying the burden of realising they need to do something to change the world, to make things better. But this is a terrible and impossible burden for any one person to bear. Likewise, those new to the path may have these heavy responsibilities tempered by the excitement of the path ahead of them. And this is precisely what they need to manifest the changes within their personal lives that will help them sustain a spiritual walk.

Many have who deep faith also struggle with the issues we are discussing here. Knowing that Life does not expect us to change the world does not help our sense of investing personal energy into making life better for others. Having a theology that Jesus or Buddha or Mohammad are in charge and Lord of All may be comforting to devout believers but even these beliefs do not diminish the human heart's sense of addressing the burdens of human suffering, discontent, lack of peace, hunger, famine and war. At the same time those who have no religious beliefs per se and may take an agnostic or atheistic approach to Life also maintain very strong ethical standards. Many activist friends and colleagues take very seriously their inner quota of responsibility for the ills of the world, and in many cases their altruism surpasses religious people by miles.

From an early age we intuitively know how we are interconnected. Human infants inspire this awareness in people all the time. Part of the innocence and beauty of childhood that we celebrate so much is this innate spiritual insight that exists prior to our adult ideas of boundaries, separations and distinctions. The transitions of youth in modern societies have largely become a time of negative forms of initiation into ways of thinking and behaving that encourage loss of hope. This is in stark contrast to older well-formed initiatory rites that highlight beliefs and values that generate hope and offer ways for youth to deal with the problems that exist in society.

One way to address these social shortfalls is to organise experiential programs that teach systems of hope, healing and personal life skills. This is an immanently practical goal and provides a long-term answer to preventing social problems before they occur. But we need more than existing models of education can offer. A threshold philosophy suggests that education needs to focus more on personal empowerment and the development of life-skills including the ability to analyse situations and engage in problem solving. Education needs to begin with the life experience of the person, the youth, the student. This is the primary data, the curriculum through which we can engage a person to seek answers that are meaningful to their own context.

Whenever people share stories of someone going to see a monk, mystic or guru you will notice that the individual leaves their familiar world for a time to go and see the teacher. But what do they bring with them? They have inside their being all the problems, concerns and life experiences that they carry. When they rock up to where the teacher lives, they show some sign of respect. They may offer food, gifts or service in exchange for personal insight. Their answers may come forward quickly or over a longer period of time depending on the nature of their search. When the change that makes the most difference occurs what is changed? The answers the seeker gets may actually lead to new and deeper questions. The insights may deal with beliefs, behaviours or an everyday practical issue. But what actually changes are the way the pilgrim thinks and feels about their problems, concerns and life experiences. The new experience of being with the teacher transforms, disintegrates, redirects, inspires, reintegrates and/or heals perception. When the seeker leaves the presence of the guru, they are in some way a new person. But the substance of what the seeker brings is hidden within their view of their world. This is what the teacher works with.

The types of healing that people are seeking in today's world often relate to changing the meaning we place on our experience. Many clients seek a more meaningful world, a place where they can have an inner sense of purpose, connection and self-worth. Other forms of healing include finding new relationship with the energy of life and a new way of living in our bodies with greater ease and balance. Meaning in our minds and in our bodies cannot be separated. All meaning is embodied.

Our minds may separate us from meaning because the way we think about things makes easy categories. Counselling is often about breaking down these perceptions of difference that block people's ability to understand their life experience. Seeing outside the boxes we build can open up new pathways. Life is rarely if ever a filing cabinet of folders where each folder represents a separate and distinct reality. Teaching people about how to access states of awareness, emotional insight and behavioural change involves learning basic life skills. We do not learn these things in school. Religious systems tend to rely on living examples of finding peace and contentment and do not teach systematic ways of accessing personal and spiritual resources. While counselling is an amazing place where people have the opportunity to learn such skills, counselling can often be expensive and inaccessible.

There are many limiting beliefs that hinder our progress toward spiritual transformation. On one hand we might hold deep-seated beliefs that we are not worthy of receiving from others or that there is something inherently wrong with receiving itself. And on the other hand, people around us may not have the same values of balancing give and take. They may even expect to take based in a belief that they deserve to get things from others without doing anything in return. A balanced spiritual-cultural system where people share common beliefs and values of giving and receiving is required for the process to become self-sustaining for everyone.

At some level it is not surprising that other people confirm the way we think about ourselves inwardly especially because we have this meaning already encoded in our minds. We affect the world around us. So, it is possible that people pick up on our state of being and they respond to us accordingly. In social environments where people do not share similar values, we need to take care. We cannot possibly give all the time and deplete our inner and outer resources without dealing with the consequences of having no energy or material objects to sustain life. In the cultures of my youth including mainstream societies and native societies there was a strong sense of the justice, fairness and reciprocity involved in each exchange of giving and receiving.

Certain people actually demand things out of the blue without even the courtesy of an introduction or building up a relationship. There is no sense of fair trade at all. Nor is there any sense of inherent respect for another person. All the people seem to see is what they want or need. Their immediate need blinds them from seeing how important relationships of mutual exchange are in their lives, and they have clearly discounted the person in front of them as outside of their sphere of respect. Within these social environments everyone remains poor because people are fundamentally locked in selfish patterns of thought that are likely based in histories of trauma, violence, abuse and disrespect.

On the other hand, there are those who acknowledge how much they receive from people and from life. They appear to have a thankful heart and go out of their way to open conversations with others that build relationships of mutual exchange. In the first instance people exchange experiences and encounters, share trade in ideas, gestures, non-verbal information and trade in objects, time and resources. Only after and during the process of building a relationship does trust tend to emerge and for some is given freely up front while for others is given only after time has passed and experiences warrant making some basic assumptions that provide a bit more ease of exchange.

We are instinctively drawn to people who have a positive outlook on life. Ironically enough, we are also repelled by positive people when we do not want to face our own negative beliefs. This is another example of how we influence our world in unconscious ways by drawing to us people who match our energy. The only way to change this pattern is by changing our inner world and by consciously choosing to be around people who have a better outlook than we do at the time. Why remain only around people who manifest problems when we can be with people who share our sense of building a world where people want to belong? There are many opportunities to be with people who are still living in the valley of discontent. We often must choose to find ways to be with people who have a vision of living life to the fullest.

Within the western tradition mendicant monks represent a strong archetype of reciprocity. These monks took vows of poverty that led them to wander the land in small groups. In exchange for helping others they begged for alms to buy a daily meal. They might sleep the night under trees, in the open air, or take shelter in a barn when that luxury came around. They gave of themselves to others by the witness of their lives. Most respectable mendicant monks worked hard for their food by doing manual labour on farms and properties.

St Francis of Assisi and his brothers gave to people in many ways including through many forms of caring for the poor and destitute, taking in the sick and staying for long periods of time tending lepers in their colonies, and offering various forms of healing, teaching, and ministry. When we have very little of material things in this world it does not mean we are spiritually poor. Indeed, in most cultural traditions the simplicity of lifestyle imposed by lack of resources encourages people to band together, to value family and relationships, work hard, and to be generous and hospitable to others as well as to depend spiritually on Creator to supply the food of the day.

At the same time spirituality suggests that when we find truth it is not helpful to hold it in isolation. We need to share our insights with others. Those on the spiritual path of integration and holistic wisdom will share in the limitations of the people around them. Spirits that are more advanced will learn lessons about life in the valley of discontent where other people are lost and engaged in habits of thought that cause harm to self and others. There is a touch of purposeful destiny in the big picture dance of life. There are many paths. And wherever you find yourself there are ways to grow.

Personal healing is possible when we are prepared to change. On many levels and in many circumstances, we can address the imbalance of our lives and correct our paths accordingly. If you've read this far it means you are committed and curious to learn about personal transformation and healing. You've already come much further than most people. Remember that being patient even when feeling the injustice of how people act is an important step in finding new insights for yourself. Accepting what other people do means you don't have to agree with them, you only need to accept and then act in your own values. In reality you cannot heal another person until they are open to change and growth. Usually healing involves some kind of letting go of an attachment emotionally and spiritually. People are not obligated to even have self-awareness. And we are not educated in these things in society.

This is part of the reason why modern medicine and health is based on objective services and not on subjective growth and wellness. We can't expect people to heal in ways that they are not open to doing and we can't even lead the horse to water nor can we force the horse to drink. This is why in the mystical teachings of many cultures the Elders do not go out and become missionaries. All the more mature traditions focus on the adept and Elder members getting on with their lives and they wait patiently for people to come around and seek out their wisdom and teachings.

When you are ready a teacher will appear because your spirit will seek them out and will manifest what your deeper self needs. Not so much what you want, but what you need will very likely appear. Otherwise, from a higher perspective your need likely looks different and it might take a bit longer to see what lies ahead. For many years the only teachers were lessons learned the hard way. And now and then the right book would appear written by mystics, priests, seers and spiritual teachers.

Eventually, it became a regular habit to read a spiritual book on a daily basis to keep something positive, helpful and challenging feeding into the mind. Healing is a parallel process to learning. They go together. Much like a person who studies herbs never gets to use all herbs in any one situation, we need to study the many types of spiritual insight, healing and knowledge so that when we need a certain skill or answer to a problem, we are more likely to be prepared.

For most of us, we just want a road map to help us get through the struggles of daily life. We'd like to have a way to understand life and death, illness and suffering, success and personal fulfilment. Naturally this book is written for those of us seeking this basic outlook on personal transformation and spirituality. And the primary message here is that you hold the keys to your mind, heart, and spirit. Enlightenment is not far away from you. The following exercise explores the themes of healing the self and others through an experiential activity. There are two parts. The first is a solitary component that you can do on your own. The second is something you can share with a partner, friend, colleague or with your therapist.

Activity 7:1 Ten Minute Spirit Meditation

When you can find ten minutes alone, sit down in a comfortable chair with good back support. Concentrate on your breathing. When you breathe in say to yourself 'Spirit of Life'. When you breathe out, say 'Love'. Focus your eyes on one spot in the room. Or close your eyes if this feels good. Do this for ten minutes. Record in your journal how you feel after the ten minutes is up. Repeat this activity at any time you wish.

Activity 7:2 Spirit Walk

Part two of this activity is to go for a walk in a park or natural setting. Do the exercise above while keeping your eyes open and observing the world around you, quietly thinking the words as you inhale and exhale… 'Spirit of Life' and… 'Love…' for the duration of your walk. When you are finished write down how you feel. Repeat this spirited walk anytime you wish. We like to call this a 'spirit-walk' and find that many people are quite astounded by their shifts of perception when they engage these skills. Now you can share the activity with someone close to you or someone you may wish to be close to. Sit together and do the first activity noted above. Instead of writing your reflections share with each other your experience. At another time go for the spirit walk together. Maintain a sense of honouring the activity and being flexible to each other's needs. Share the experience afterwards over a cuppa or bring a picnic lunch with you into the park.

Stardust Awakens

8 Centre: Power to Change the World

Centring, still point, spirals dance

Creation awaits her lover

Trees, stones, lakes, the moss

Be at peace, all is not lost

Power to change, to give away

When we enter the path of spiritual power, we ought to expect some resistance. Like Franchesca Cabrini, who founded numerous hospitals and charities throughout the East coast of the USA, coming to terms with this resistance is very important. Spiritual powers tend bring alive the grains of everyday material life. What at first feels like resistance is really the shifting of vibrational energies. By moving at a much faster frequency, spiritual power shakes up reality and realigns our priorities. This is exactly why the higher realms of spiritual commitment require in some ways the letting go of attachments to the material world, even while embracing this very world with compassion and love. This is also why spiritual emergence often first appears like crisis

– we get shaken up by the powerful forces of divine energy. We can no longer stay the same. We have to change; we have no choice. We can either move forward or take several steps backwards. In either of these cases we in fact change enormously. Change is not a choice we make – we can only respond to the change. If we are wise, we will go with the flow of spiritual emergence.

Spiritual energy is amazing and mysterious. One form of energy is slow and obtuse – our material world. This too is spiritual but vibrates at a slower pace. Everything and everyone consist of Life Energy. The other form of energy is fast and subtle – our immaterial world.

Spiritual power is so vastly powerful that it crosses time and space in a flash. There are no spatial or temporal boundaries placed on spiritual energy. Even the speed of light is merely a material phenomenon that is surpassed by spiritual energy.

There are Old Laws that govern spiritual powers that predate human existence and that are grounded in the Earth World and move across the Many Worlds of existence. These Laws are based in ethics and the balance of the Sacred Worlds. These laws are very different from that which governs the world of women and men. We are also wise to learn these Old Ways, as this knowledge assists us in managing the rocky roads of spiritual growth and transformation.

It never ceases to amaze that when people want to change, the closest people in their lives tend to resist change even though they want the best for their loved one or co-worker. Especially when the changes may influence the people around us in positive ways, everyone seems to be slightly changed fatigued.

It often takes time for us to inform and nurture openness to change in our family, friends and colleagues. When we are moving forward most of us want our community to come along with us. No change happens in isolation, and it is very sad when change separates people unnecessarily. Spiritual energy is also working its mystery in these social contexts.

People are motivated in different ways. Some want to create new visions, others want to maintain stability, some wish to manage systems that already exist, while certain people find their meaning in creating and changing systems. There are people who want to relate, and they focus on the process of emotional sharing. Others see how making decisions moves events forward, so their motivation grows when they focus on the decision-making tasks of the day. Some see the bigger picture while others feel comfortable doing the physical aspects of getting the job done.

Like the Christian scriptures suggest, each contribution is part of the one body of people. The head is no more important than the feet or the hands. All these skills and capabilities are manifestations of the power to change the world.

In a similar way, we all travel at different speeds. Not everyone is destined to vibrate at the higher spiritual levels at which powerful forms of healing and manifesting of human transformation tends to occur. However, we are on the journey. So, we all need to know how to manage spiritual emergence.

One key to negotiating change with our family, friends and colleagues is through understanding that everyone tends to have different sources of motivation. If we can figure out what areas provide motivation for others, we can more readily direct our actions to build a bridge of understanding with that person.

Everyone is motivated by fear and/or pleasure. Many managers know this, and instilling fear is a common technique to bring people's productivity in line. Not the best management style. Fear based motivation creates fatigue. It is not sustainable. It does not bring people forward over the long term nor does it create a world where people want to belong. Pleasure based motivation is about finding ways to live and work together that provide inspiration, greater confidence and mutual respect. This sounds great but it is not easy.

Having motivation to achieve great things and to create the best program or the best outcome may drive a person to act quickly and speak openly. Sometimes words can challenge and affect people in ways you don't anticipate. Instead of seeing a positive motivation people in their states of change-fatigue and caution to new ideas will see words as threatening, rather than with intention to inspire. This is an amazing and strange phenomenon. But when you look more deeply, the people who experience these responses have invested much energy over time in creating the world as it is now. They may not want to change!

When you come along with new ideas of how to improve people's lives they do not always go, 'Oh great, I was just sitting here waiting for someone like you to come along and change everything!' Catching the irony of this statement, many people don't want to change. They fear spiritual power for this very reason. Instead, people who are invested in the way the world looks to them today will see your efforts as offensive. Indeed, they will look at their own hard work over the years to create what already exists. They will not see a need to change. They will not welcome change or new ideas. When someone shows up with ideas to change the world people often feel like they are being critiqued, challenged and are less than adequate.

To really make change possible we need to understand how to inspire change that matters not only to us, but also for those around us. We have come to understand that every idea for change can only succeed in the short term if it has a ready context for fulfilment. People must want to embrace the change. Otherwise it will not succeed in the long term.

Change is also more easily communicated when there is some distance from applying change to everyday life and workplace circumstances. For example, couple retreats away from home or training programs in the workplace that are conducted off-site can provide a neutral ground for people to consider change. In home family therapy and workplace-based programs can sometimes be more confronting, but the rationale is that people will get more from applying the change directly to existing practices. Only when families and/or professionals are oriented toward these more radical forms of self-critique and self-examination will these interventions work effectively. Even then, people can be defensive and resist change.

The best changes happen because people want them. The key to be a successful person in society is to figure out what changes people want and to deliver the context in which these changes can be manifested. But to be the best human being we can be, first we need to discover what we really want out of life. A great deal of self-reflection is necessary.

But conversely, no reflection at all is needed to know that spiritual life is good, and that we ought to walk this path. Something inside the majority of people doesn't even need to switch on. We just know. If we have an opportunity to learn and grow, most of us will jump at it. We have an innate sense that these kinds of moments come once in a lifetime. The spiritual path is very much like this.

Accepting opportunities as they arise can lead you down many roads that will enrich your life to no end. If you stay put, remain in fear, keep yourself contained in self-doubt, very few of these new experiences are likely to happen for you. This is not to say that remaining in one place might also be your destiny, and new vistas of awareness could well be hidden inside your life that you have not yet acknowledged.

There are so many models of accomplishment out there. But as much as we might focus on finding solutions, answers and action plans, we all must acknowledge that we learn best through our mistakes. Adult life at its best is about making helpful and nurturing compromises that work to sustain life over the long term. If we do not have a sustainable lifestyle and a sustainable psychology, we will not last long. While we are busy maintaining the systems we work in, we may still access the spirit of youth that guided us to where we are now. Our original youthful and childhood visions have much to offer us by way of inspiration and direction.

Not enough attention is given to mid-career transitions. What happens for people when they find the job they wanted, but they find themselves working in the wrong place? Maybe they cannot fulfil their dreams while they work in overly negative, self-limiting and dysfunctional environments. In my view we find ourselves in such places to learn important lessons. Every person makes many mistakes. No one is immune. We all have limiting beliefs that we need to examine and overcome. A spice of humility may be in order as well.

What about when a person finds the keys to change in their work environment, but they feel unfulfilled in their relationships? This often happens for men and women nowadays after investing so heavily in career and family development for the first half of life. Mid-life crisis has a parallel with mid-career transitions for many important reasons. How we make our sense of meaning, our spirituality, has a lot to do with mid-life crisis. If we have not made a sustainable framework for meaning in our lives, we will feel the need to address this shortfall in mid-life.

For those of us who have invested in creating meaning most of our lives the mid-life transition may involve different levels of searching. Many people who have created meaningful worlds find that later, during their mid-life, they become much more focused in manifesting the energies of healing, growth and transformation in their work and their personal lives.

Once you know any truth intellectually it is time to manifest that truth in actions. Learning happens both ways. But since you are reading this book you have reflected much at an intellectual level. You have taken time to experience insight and emotions through the activities in this text, but your work here has been primarily intellectual. It is ironic to say that many of our best answers cannot rely on the intellect alone.

Our conscious minds are limited in their capacity to solve problems and to create new possibilities. This is in part why we so highly recommend the activities combined with the practice of self-reflection through journal writing. This changes the energy of the intellect into action, and by engaging in the process of change itself you are manifesting a spiritual discipline. This will in turn open up life-giving energies that will assist you to manifest the changes that Creator wishes for your life.

Learning to work with our minds for a change is also very important. Our conscious minds are focusing mechanisms. We can focus consciously on 1 to 4 bits of information at once on a good day. But most of the time our cognitive mind is transiting between focuses so that we may be aware of driving the car, maintaining a conversation, the actions of other drivers, the music on the radio and our stiff back – all in intermittent and transitory ways.

Our awareness is shifting all the time, but we are primarily focused on our thoughts and the environment around us. Our unconscious mind is closer to body awareness. As well, all our memories and collective experiences are stored in our unconscious and body-systems.

By learning how to access this hidden resource we can find new tools for problem solving and creative living. Learning to work with our minds for a change is an important part of the picture that many of us overlook. For instance, how much easier it is to trust the unconscious mind.

At night-time, when worries are pounding away, you may often say a meditation to your unconscious and a prayer to Creator. While reflecting on the issues of the day you may give these to your unconscious and creative self. There is only so much we can do in any one day, and the rest we must let go of. We cannot hold on. If we do, our lives will become unsustainable and we will self-destruct.

When you let go of the day, you are able to sleep with peace and assurance. When you wake up, new energy and vitality will be yours.

The problems of the old day will be gone, and some will need to be addressed in new and fresh ways. This discipline of mind has given us a new lease on life after years of living with chronic stress and unsolved issues, most of which were the problems of other people internalised into our own experience. Learning to trust how the body is already set up to find solutions and deal with problems is really so important. No one teaches this stuff, and that never ceases to amaze!

By understanding the subtle energies of our unconscious mind-body we can better facilitate health and learn the skills of maintaining boundaries. Almost everyone has a difficulty with boundaries. It seems universal. This is expressed in hundreds of ways.

For example: By taking on more work than we should and not taking care of our physical health. By pushing work on a colleague without attention to the consequences in their lives. By taking on the emotions and problems of people around us, not helping ourselves in the process and doing little good for friends, family or colleagues. Dumping our issues on others. Giving our energy away or taking on the energy of another too much. Being abusive, disrespectful or controlling of another person's life. Allowing ourselves to be pushed around too easily. Physically violating another's space. Disrespecting our own bodies and violating principles of health and emotional wellness through all sorts of activities. These are only a few examples of boundary issues.

Intuitive and psychic boundaries are just as important. The obvious levels of this relate to emotional boundaries. People tend to have learned emotional responses to various stimuli. Over time emotional patterns emerge. At the psychic level the intuitive energies of personal boundaries are more difficult to discern.

For example, we often describe a person's 'presence' as manifesting certain psychic qualities like peace or hyper-activity. These intuitive states are more pervasive in the personality than emotional states, which tend to come and go over time. Emotional and psychic states can come to define a person's spirit. They can become associated with the energies of spiritual powers and presences they unconsciously welcome into their circle. Old family patterns reveal this well. We take on the unresolved issues of our parents, grandparents and further back in the chain. When in an intuitive state it is possible to sense the spiritual presence of a person and the energies that are attached or linked to them. If you compare these insights with other people, there is often overlap and congruence between what is sensed. These verifications point to another way of testing intuitive insight.

It is often said that we are what we eat. In a similar way we become what we feel most, over time. If your energies are dominated by states of anger, frustration, control and anxiety, one or more of these combinations will come to characterise your psychic energy. Your 'spirit' as it were will come to express these energies and draw other energies of similar value into your sphere of influence. You will manifest these energies in ever more efficient and systematic ways. The same is true for energies of peace, love, kindness and happiness. You will also manifest in your spirit the energy of a place, like the city or the natural environment where you live.

Many of us are spiritually in-tune at the core, but we have a lot of garbage covering our spirits. We are not free to be ourselves, to fulfil our destiny or to know how to find our energies and take the path to fulfilment. We have never learned to trust our intuition. We do not listen to the still small voice inside us and instead we listen too much to the voices of parents, family and society who tell us how to live our lives. Our personal boundaries are almost non-existent in these cases. Our 'self' has never been developed and so we have collapsed boundaries that allow the world to invade us and dominate our lives. Learning to change the world in these cases is to first come to terms with our psychic energies. To see clearly where we have come from, and then to make changes in our emotional lives that help us take the next step.

A central realisation for everyone is that you are more than what you feel. Our feelings are not our core identities. Underneath our feelings and emotions is a psychic being, an intelligence, a core self. And underneath this is a spiritual energy that is tapped into Life and Universal Essence. Most of us think we are standing on the physical earth. But the reality of life in this cosmos is that we are grounded in a fluid spiritual quantum that is forever evolving. In this fluid universe our psychic presence, our emotions, our physical bodies and our environments are all floating in this sea of being. The physical world is our greatest illusion. Real life is much more spiritual than we have yet discovered.

Changing the world is really about Creating with Life a Spiritual Energetic Shift that unites human consciousness to universal energies of evolution. This is a profoundly spiritual task.

Divine Life is evolving with us. We are a community of being who is one with the Creator of Being. Doing a good job today at work, making bread for the family or doing the dishes after you cook a decent meal are just as important acts if they are done with an awareness of giving.

Transformation is not restricted to the therapy room in this way of looking at life. Every act we do today constitutes possible links in the chain of our becoming manifest beings of light, love and universal justice.

Intuition tells us that many people on the planet today are much closer to Manifest Life than most of us realise. Manifest Life is a way of understanding the mindset and states of being that Jesus, Mohammad, Buddha and other Great Beings experienced. We indeed stand on this very threshold.

The human community is evolving at ever increasing rates. War and social discord are equally significant signs of a transitional struggle in consciousness that disrupts people's core values, cultures and sense of security. While one cause to this human suffering is obviously economic and physical, in the spiritual realm there is a collective awakening that challenges the way people live.

Indeed, these changes increase the likelihood of discontent, social upheaval and conflict, especially when people are not aware of the underlying transformations that are being asked of us. Environmental changes are a perfect example.

We can no longer afford to stay the same and live the same lifestyles that assume too much and take even more. A trans-cultural ethic is emerging globally rooted in ancient principles of ecological sustainability. Even while this change is positive on one hand, there are many today who suffer and live in poverty in part because of these very issues that are driving the economy and political life. The spread of virus in this global village is inevitable, and the ways that people have become settled in mass numbers within small apartment buildings and retirement villages is terribly problematic. Modern life is not sustainable at the best of times; and pity the lot of us during the hardest of times.

When considering these issues, we tend to think that the 'end times' suggested in the last book of the Christian New Testament is a spiritual metaphor worth thinking about. Endings are inevitable. Human societies tend to grow to a point and then decline, new cycles emerge, and transformations occur.

We are now facing the last cycle in a larger spiral of human development that goes back thousands of years. During the last parts of any cycle we manifest spiritual awakening that transforms our whole existence. Last cycles speak of autumn, death, letting go, and regeneration, taking stock and making amends.

During ending phases of life wisdom transforms our worldview, and actions become grounded in manifest being. A holistic and integrative perspective emerges. This is the life stage of the Elder. At this level we are more in touch with psychic and spiritual insight and there is an increase of higher capacities for manifesting healing, extrasensory insight and transpersonal experience.

Whatever becomes the highest level of development tends to reorient and reintegrate the former developmental stages. Where mid-life crisis tends to address forgotten parts of us that were not developed, the emergence of psychic and spiritual cycles sometimes creates major renovations in the whole person. This is often experienced as crisis, but the underlying results are deeply healing.

In these developments, change manifests in different ways because the meaning placed on actions has more pervasive, enduring and humanitarian significance. All of the most important and enduring social movements started with one person and sometimes one person within a small group of individuals who had a vision.

This is our essential power to change the world. When we take our personal vision quest seriously, the Spirit of Life gives us experiences that change us to the core. We re-enter life; and the small 'I' transforms with a changed perspective.

Likewise, whenever we intentionally cleanse our body through fasting and prayer and when we take time in solitude to seek the Spirit for guidance, we allow clarity and deeper peace to guide our actions. Fasting is a way to cleanse the body and spirit. Fasting can mean any form of changing our diet to intentionally seek a higher form of energy. Fasting is most helpful when eating only fresh veggies and fruit with lots of natural juices and water. Others fast by eating bread and drinking only water. Eating most of today's carbs does not help the body to cleanse from toxins and carbs tend to work best while gaining weight. Everyone has a different experience.

But this central ability to vision, to experience now what the world ought to be like at its best, this is the heart and spirit of all the mechanisms of change. All of our energy should lead us to creating and nurturing a personal body-mind space, a Sacred Space that can become fully attuned to Life and Truth.

Being well grounded in personal Sacred Space is the only way we can sustain a long-term confrontation of the demons of destruction and social disease that are threatening our way of life on earth. We do not want to become burned out and lose the war on terror because ultimately this is a spiritual warfare that is being waged across nations, cultures and religions. My metaphors of the end times here are used to dramatic effect. Within us are forces of Light and Shadow, to be sure, and we each need to find a way to bring the balance into these Sacred Times on our Planet.

Unlike many people suggest, current global challenges are not about national, cultural or religious issues per se. Underneath these surface problems is a more sustained conflict around the assumptions people have about controlling people's minds and hearts – but ultimately, we can control nothing. In fact, humanity is evolving. And this is the underlying spiritual transformation of this era.

At the end of the day each and every person must choose his or her path in life. If you choose the path of anger, frustration, aggression and violence you will manifest these qualities in life. If you choose the path of love, peace, responsibility, nurturance, justice and mercy you will also manifest these qualities in life. Both paths are spiritual. But only the latter path of Light and Being brings humanity to our ultimate destiny.

In the end only love, faith and hope exist for eternity. This is the way of existence and non-existence because these words represent the essential energies of Creation that govern the cosmic forces of evolution. Darkness and destruction are only a shadow, instantly integrated into the energy of light. Fear also ceases to exist because the energy of fear is a servant of the Light, a mere pathway into the Light.

We might also say that faith, hope and love are the DNA of existence while all the other experiences only provide a backdrop and an elusive fluid for the primary consciousness to proceed. We might remember the Yin/Yang symbol. But what people forget or fail to see is that in the final analysis both sides of the yin-yang disappear into Being.

Once the Circle starts spinning at spiritual velocity, all that actually remains is a spiral. The DNA spiral exists in the balanced integration of light and dark. In this final moment of Being, opposites cease to exist and all that remains is the pure intention of Being. This Being does not say I am good, or I am evil. The final word does not say I am faith, hope or love. The final utterance merely says, 'I AM.' This voice expresses the western mystical tradition's finest insight.

You can experience these realities in so many ways. Being is a purity of awareness that can happen simply by closing the eyes and breathing deeply. Remember that your breath, in this moment, in this now, is the very Thread of Life that sustains your body. You are your breath. What does this mean?

As you sit with eyes closed, put your feet on the floor, or sit on the ground outside if that is possible. Feel the earth under your feet or under your behind. Draw in the energy of your breathing. If you were to stop breathing your spirit would have to eventually leave your body. Your body would expire. The purity of Being is now in your breath, breathing in and then letting go.

This cycle continues regardless how you feel, where you are, how much money you have, if you are well educated or just a simple kind of person. Your breath is your life force and defines a part of your identity as a living, sentient being. When doing this exercise, you might be profoundly moved and look inside the self and see the darkness behind your closed eyes and imagine the stars of the night sky. You might think and feel, *I am stardust*. But you are conscious and alive! It blows the heart and mind into a million pieces to awaken from the sleep of darkness. Then, you are all but quiet, listening… and all you can hear is your breathing…

Being and non-being are then one.
I realise that "I" does not exist.
What exists is the great expanse.
All that "I" have become is but a small fragment.
A tiny part of the vast beautiful cosmos.

I am more than what I feel.
More than what I think.
I am the arising in conscious awareness
That comes and goes in a flash
Like a wave upon the sea
Or a flicker of a distant star.
My identity ceases to exist.
A tiny molecules of water;
Only a fragment of the wave
Washed out to sea.

'Being' as an experience, in this way, when fully embraced, often leads to profound realisations of our natural place within the cosmos. Often, we are quite surprised if not dismayed at how humbling things really are, when we strip away ego and persona, and find what truth exists beyond our self-importance.

This says a lot about the dark side, and what intensity of illusion sustains the notions of power and will to harm. What most chronically warring peoples, terrorists, neo-Nazis, fundamentalists, death-fixated suicide bombers and hard-line capitalists have in common is an attachment to human suffering. This chronic attachment is sustained to the exclusion of healing or transformation.

Ego-identity and self-importance have become so twisted and out of proportion to the spiritual reality, that people become extremely lost. In certain cases, personal gains outweigh the common good. In other cases, ideological warfare over an elusive control of people's minds had long ago taken over any rational means to find solutions. For still others emotional disturbance and horrific circumstances drive destructive agendas that continue a chronic cycle of war, death and trauma.

But regardless how terrible things have become around the world, circumstances may get worse before they get better. The reason for this is that we call into our lives what we will to manifest through our habits of thought. We share this energy with another, and they come to share the same train of thought. Simple physics. But profoundly disturbing to realise how much power each of us actually has to influence the course of history.

At this time in our collective story we are sharing more and more the intention to heal, learn and grow. And this ought to be celebrated and encouraged. The science of personal transformation attends closely to issues of empowerment, working through emotions and associations created by violation and creating intention and sustainable mental and emotional worldviews.

Healing from many issues is the work and focus of counselling psychotherapy even while helping people attain their personal and social goals. But a holistic approach that involves spiritual insights certainly adds much to the mix that otherwise remains hidden.

Activity 8 Manifesting, Empowering

Finding what we want in life is the first and last key to spiritual growth. No progress is made unless we are able to listen, attend to our inner voice, and receive the information from Life within us – and then choose what we want to do. At every turn in the journey we are asked to take these first steps. It never changes.

We are looking, seeking, knocking and searching for the way forward. It often feels like we are in the dark, we don't know where to turn. But Life gives us the answers we need when we listen carefully.

This is why this book is ended with a very simple and practical activity. Don't be fooled by the simplicity. Even the most advanced spiritual practitioner will take the same steps at a different level of being, maybe with a new focus, but the same principles apply.

In the spiritual realms we need to cut through all our personality issues, fears and anxieties, and find what is true in the deepest part of ourselves. Only then can we find the pearl of great price. That treasure is self-awareness made manifest into a practical and meaningful life in the world.

Bringing these worlds together in pragmatic ways is the purpose of spiritual enlightenment. There is little sense in evolving alone. Indeed, when one spirit awakens the whole cosmos ripples with excitement.

This exercise focuses on career and vocational choices as the example of finding your inner most desires. But you can actually explore other ways of doing this, like looking for your core values in life, or seeking your vision quest sense of what the Creator wants for you.

The reasons we stay with the 'mundane' issues of jobs and careers is that, at least during the first half of the human lifespan, and very likely during the second, we ground a lot of our spiritual choices in the everyday worlds of work. To bring a deeper discernment, searching and spiritual awareness to this world is very important. This brings greater health and balance to our lives.

To find what you really want in life ask yourself, 'What did I want when I was a child?'

Childhood dreams hold enormous power because of the purity and lack of self-interest involved in dreaming during that time of our lives. List out the things you dreamed of doing when you grew up. Write these in your journal. When you have these down, ask yourself why did I want this? What was I hoping to achieve?

Don't stop with the obvious. Keep going deeper and try to map out in circles around the dream the different ways that that dream fulfils needs and roles in your life and the lives of others.

Remember that dreams are a way of tapping into our unconscious, and this also is another pathway to uncovering the mind of the Creator for us. Although we need to take care.

Dreams can also bring up unresolved issues, problems, and relational difficulties. These can teach us much about what needs work and may provide clues about how to resolve certain issues.

Bringing this content to a psychotherapist may be a good idea, as getting someone else's view of things often helps. Discussing with a trusted other tends to release energy and uncover hidden meanings we would never think of otherwise.

These underlying associations that you uncover often hold the keys to positive changes and adaptations. Once we have new awareness, then we are free to make more informed choices and to move on with life.

If you wanted one thing when you dreamed of life as a child, your answers will be much easier to understand. But if you are like me and you wanted a hundred million things in life, you will have to do more work to decide what is the most essential part of your desires.

If your goals were many like mine, you may find yourself going from one thing to another over the years without really feeling fulfilled. One part of you is fulfilled doing this job, but other parts are not. It may take many years to sort through the desires of your heart. And then you realise that you were never meant to fulfil your inner purpose in any one situation, job or circumstance. Indeed, you begin to accept that life actually is a journey not a destination.

This being true, still, we all need to find work and activities that give us some degree of satisfaction. To get there we need to match our capabilities in life and our desires with job and career options and attempt to find the best-fit possible. Every career has its ups and downs, and this is common right across the board. What we are seeking is the greatest degree of freedom to accomplish most of our essential goals. But to find this answer, we first need to clarify our goals.

Take the list of what you want to accomplish from each dream of childhood and/or youth and the jobs or careers you generate from those dreams. In column two list the essential part of the job for you. To get the answer you need for this column, ask yourself 'If I had these things to the fullest, what will that really do for me?'

You may find yourself surprised by the answers that come up. They may be things you never thought of before and will shed new light on the underlying needs and desires that motivate your decisions in jobs and career.

Also, you might find that even the most seemingly 'mundane' jobs hold quite amazingly spiritual intentions at the heart. For example, below I use a childhood dream of my own to be truck driver. The outcomes of this job when I ask, 'If I had these things to the fullest, what will that really do for me?' relate to the ability to move the earth, to change the world for the better, and to create beautiful places to be. This dream led me personally to explore landscape gardening as one option that didn't become a career move but was indeed expressed as a personal hobby. As I reflected on the deeper meanings, the metaphors of moving the earth and opening change in the world looked like parallels to my teaching and healing work with others. But the reality is, if I had become a truck driver as a profession, I may still have come to the same place spiritually. Our core intentions have a way of manifesting regardless what specific path in life we choose.

When you realise what a job will give you, you can see more clearly that you can actually find these rewards in many different careers. Other jobs can be maintained as hobbies and secondary sources of income as well. So, by narrowing down, we may decide to keep things that mean a lot to us. Helpful to realise that a bit of solid career discernment and vocational decision-making can save many years of struggle and lots of time and money.

Many people are called to be a mother or father. This act is encoded in our bodies, minds and identities. Many others feel called to not have children for various reasons, or the circumstance of not being able to have children is thrust upon them. Whether coming from a deep sense of vocation or being almost forced to accept our lot in life, people's paths lead them to similar places – towards deep abiding self-awareness and personal transformation. Whether the path arises from negative or positive energies or experiences does not matter as much as the choices that we make along the way.

Are you on the right path in life? Or do you feel the need for change? What changes would make the most sense to you now? How would each change fit within your life-ecology, the environment of your family, your relationships and contexts of your life and work?

When you imagine opening yourself to the divine intention for your life, what do you imagine the Creator wants for you? What does the creation around you speak to your inner self – in your dreams, in your fantasies, in your creative daydreaming? Being more aware of these movements within and around you can open up many important insights.

You might ask: Do I choose to open my mind and heart to new insight and awareness? Do I continue to seek more understanding? Or do I decide to close myself from life, hiding from uncomfortable realisations? Write in your journal and share your questions and reflections with a friend.

Take a moment to pause and reflect on the ways that you have manifested the power of your spirit, your energy, into your daily life. Consider for a moment that your early childhood dreams and visions were part of this energy attempting to manifest ideas and insights into the world of material forms. As you grew over the years your manifest life continued to unfold. At times you learned to cover your light, and hide behind a tree, as if you may have revealed too much to others around you. At other times you may have been a beacon of light in your world, excited to share your talents and insights with others. Now as you are intentionally reflecting on the spiritual path, consider making an inner commitment to the practice of Manifest Life by taking promises in your innermost being.

If you were to really manifest divine life in the world, what would you seek to bring into life and being? Now apply this question to your life, career, job and work in the world. Include your family in this overall sense of service. What would you want to bring to this world by way of energy? Purpose? Destiny? If you were to make vows or promises in your spirit to walking this spiritual way, what might they look like? Would you make promises of bringing peace, compassion, love, forgiveness, blessing or truth into the world?

Consider for a time these values, and what you wish to manifest in your spirit – and consider that you might be making a commitment in the Spirit World that could be witnessed by hundreds and thousands of other Higher Beings, Elders, Teachers, Guides, Prophets, and Manifest Beings of Light. If you were to humbly kneel in that Ancient Circle in the Chamber of Ancient Beings, what promises would you make? Who would be standing in front of you, accepting your vows for all eternity, witnessed by the Ancient Ones who Live?

Would the Ancient Gum Trees of Australia stand also as witness? Might the Mighty Oak and Hemlock of the Northern Woods of Turtle Island or North America come to provide strength and stability to your quest? Would the Spirit of the Eagle, Wolf, Bear and Turtle come to Protect and Guide your work in the Earth World and across all the Sacred Worlds? Would the Seven Sacred Directions of the Circle and the Four Quarters of the Cross of the Cosmic Christ arise to give you comfort, strength and power?

In whatever ways you imagine your spirit walk to occur, consider now that even in a silent wish upon a star there are hidden and mysterious happenings in the world. Sometimes all a spirit can do is whisper the unspoken words in the heart. Sometimes even this is too much. Even just reading these words might echo an ancient song from eons ago, from your distant Ancestors who lived in caves and upon the open plains or the deep forests of the post ice age.

In that memory from within our human tribal bloodlines, we all, everyone on this planet, are bound by the ethics of respect, honour, balance, humility, learning, listening and awakening that form the Seven Directions we have explored during this study. Within these energies of the Old Law the idea of promises is already made, manifest in the Ancient Dreaming and the Sacred Medicine traditions of our Elders. We have only to sit upon Mother Earth and be still. Breathe deeply. Allow our lives to unfold. And be true to our inner voice. These are our paths to enlightenment.

Conclusion

Spiritual practice holds the keys to self-awareness, but the cost of transformation needs to be faced head on. We cannot expect to advance in higher degrees of spiritual life unless we are willing to face our fears, uncertainties and weaknesses. When we are in the midst of these challenges it feels like there is no future. We feel trapped by our own limited perspectives. We even think that we might have to give up too much to attain a spiritual life. In this we are wrong – for every spiritual path in life opens up choices and allows us to take on more than what we have now. But facing these fears is still important. And many people get stuck here for years without taking their journey any further.

But spiritual life is structured exactly this way. We see in front of us what we need to see right now. Right here and now is all we get. Creator does not want us to see too far ahead when what we need to understand is right in front of us. This is why we are trapped, by thinking what is happening right now is all there is in life. This way of thinking holds many people firmly in a very limited now. Especially youth. When youth get stuck in this place they tend to start thinking about self-harming behaviours. If all I have is what exists now, then there is no future for me. This is an illusion that passes once we face our demons and build up a bit of inner strength and esteem. Only afterwards do we see the bigger picture.

Then we can look back and awaken to what was really going on when we faced that terrible challenge or dark place in the past. Jobs and careers, the people we meet each day, and the reasons why we are where we are today come down to opening up spiritual doorways that can lead us to our destiny. We can come to understand why so many people deny the power of destiny, precisely because they have never had the courage nor the faith or vision to come to terms with their own purpose in life. They would prefer that everyone stay stuck in their own dull version of the world. At least then there would be no more challenges to their way of being.

Many ask, why should Creator open up spiritual worlds to those who do not desire to work for their enlightenment? Even Jesus told his disciples to not bother throwing pearls to the pigs who would not bother to listen or take heed to his teachings. It sounds like a harsh thing to say.

Yes, the fact of the matter is that not everyone is interested in personal transformation and spiritual awakening. We can easily respect this fact and move on to other people who are willing to collaborate. But at the same time, our vows to attain universal human enlightenment also involve carrying compassion for pigs, ugly ducklings, stray dogs, and rabid wolves. While having strong boundaries, this spiritual vision embraces every sentient and non-sentient being, every rock, stone and tree. We are all one family of creation straining toward enlightenment.

When you contemplate your personal decisions on jobs and careers some of the process is quite practical and mundane. We pick the work we feel we can do best. But people also appear to be almost driven toward certain vocations like the arts, health or helping others, caring or supportive roles. A tiny touch of destiny comes to play in many career and life decisions. And still others are drawn to practical and hands-on work, but this too expresses a deeper sense of self and identity.

Within these core intentions arise equally compelling spiritual choices that open up pathways towards manifest life. In a Christian way of speaking, we open ourselves to Creator's will for our lives and by doing so, our path transforms us into what Life intends for us. The Goddess manifests within us a power to create and influence the lives of others through our devotion, faith and acts of kindness.

Many jobs, careers and paths in life overlap. Over time we can become many things and do even more than we ever imagined. The key is to stay open minded and to learn to attend to your heart – your inner voice – and heed the messages you hear that lead you to health and wellness. Most people today have three or four major 'careers' and often call these lifetimes that are unique and separated by a time-space dimension linked to major life changes.

Remember that your personal journal can be your best friend. Be creative and consider expanding the nature of your journal activity. In ancient times and today the Medicine Bundle was a memory devise when people did not have a means to write. Each item in the bundle holds a memory of divine inspiration and guidance. With the advent of writing many cultures recorded information of spiritual and cultural significance on stone, strips of birch bark, beadwork, and later on parchment, paper and pen.

Today many people also use the laptop and handheld devises as a way to record the spiritual and personal journey in life. Blogs have also become a significant form of writing daily thoughts and insights while sharing them with others. The practice has many therapeutic and social functions. Whatever tools you decide to use, the basic life-skills offered throughout this book give you a foundation for endless growth while manifesting your potential. By tapping into your deeper intentions towards life-choices you have one of the most important keys to unfolding your unique life-story. So, at this time, as we conclude this book, we ask you to remember the various skills and lessons learned throughout this book during the activities in each chapter.

In chapter one you reflected on your personal story and the major touchstones on your life path. You looked at who were your inspiring voices, mentors or guides. And then you reflected on what you wanted to experience in life during the future, where you wanted to be in five- or ten-years' time.

In chapter two, you focused on building the skills of keeping a personal journal. You entered into basic meditation exercises focused on breathing slowly and steady. Becoming quiet and peaceful. Then posing an inner question to the Sacred Silence, and remaining quiet and calm, waiting with patience and openness to whatever answers come up. And then you recorded these in your journal. You also explored celebrating your personal story including family heritage, cultural origins and personal development and change over the years.

In chapter three, you began a process of examination of conscience by looking in detail at your actual daily routines and activities, in order to explore where you are placing your energy. Then you examined these and explored what things you do that might not be so helpful, while looking at other things you felt might be better for you in the long run. These skills allowed you to make more informed choices. Additionally, in chapter three you generated a dream list of things you'd love to do some time in future. Then you sorted through the list. All of these activities combined core self-care life-skills that assist people to gain self-awareness and to manifest the energy of Life.

In chapter four, you collected stones and opened a place of sanctuary in a circle. You explored the physical space around and next to your body and reclaimed your personal space as sacred and important. You opened more awareness of the energies you carry around with you, and then had some choices about what to do with these energies. You learned skills of cleansing energy in your body and around you, and the spaces you occupy. You learned how your energy relates to the world around you, like how you fill the space of the circle and the room, and how you can project your energy or contain it close and hidden next to your body.

Then you learned about your personal boundaries, their history, place and purpose in your life and in relationships. Then you took the stones and opened a Circle, exploring the various directions and learning skills of thanksgiving, personal awareness, communication, and observation. From there you learned about working with personal issues in the safe space of the circle. You learned to observe the issue, form a more direct and conscious relationship to the issue, and to engage in therapeutic change processes with that issue that might open up new awareness, detachment and objectivity. These allowed you to have more choices around how to work with problems.

In chapter five, you entered back into the process of examining time spent during your past week on various tasks, and then on ways to improve your lifestyle to fit within your deeper values. You explored the idea of personal space and the notion of taking a retreat as a time for personal reflection and perhaps also solitude. You also engaged in discussing and planning a retreat experience with your partner and family, and perhaps even took the plunge and did a personal retreat that was suited to your own needs.

In chapter six, you explored sensory skills of observation and picking up subtle sensory awareness. You entered into strategies to help build intuitive abilities.

In chapter seven, you engaged a meditation based on the breath using the words 'Spirit of Life' when taking air inside your lungs, and "Love" when exhaling. You focused on a spot in the room or closed your eyes. You tried to do this for ten minutes. If you felt it might be helpful you may have decided to do this activity once or twice a day. Then you learned the skill of doing a spirit-walk meditation. Sharing this with a friend was very likely a special and worthwhile experience.

In chapter eight, you explored again the notions of personal life-choices, vocation and career in order to consolidate the learning throughout this book and to manifest more directly your desires, hopes and dreams in sync with your beliefs and values, and the Divine Intention. The underlying challenge to manifest in your working life the desire of your spirit was at the heart of this activity. You also explored a review of the activities and skills learned during your journey through this book.

Speaking the underlying intentions behind these activities, by empowering the Spirit to manifest into daily life, and into the mundane worlds of career, job, work and family life, we complete the Sacred Circle began in Chapter one, thus bringing us back to the beginning.

Connecting the teachings, what we have shared with daily life makes the tasks of this book meaningful and purposeful.

Enlightenment is embodied in your daily practice, your work, your life, and your loving.

Re-reading your journal entries during this journey may be a good way to touch base with the different experiences, and to draw some conclusions for yourself while looking at where to go next. Each of these activities represents a new threshold of personal transformation and self-therapy.

These stepping-stones provide the basis for spiritual awakening, the latter not being something otherworldly, but rather is a practical growth in your capacity as a human being. Whenever we talk about the spiritual life, we are straddling two worlds – the mundane and the mystical. Combined are the ordinary and the extraordinary.

Spirituality, you will remember, is about how we make our sense of meaning in the world. Mysticism is about how we experience spirituality. Spiritual awakening is an essential component of human capacities, because spirituality involves our becoming more mature adults, entering the place of wisdom, generosity, altruism and service to others.

Our western world and the professions do people a great disservice when suppressing and denying such an important layer of human evolution and development. By incorporating the skills, teachings, and insights within this book we go a long way to opening up and nurturing human potential.

In this way, this book has provided activities that represent an essential part of ancient and modern initiation experiences. Every person could benefit from this knowledge, awareness and level of skill because these abilities provide greater capacity to face life's challenges and to navigate the harsh realities of sickness, disease, hardship, relationship breakdown, and the death of a loved one. Having skills in being a spiritually aware person with maturity, integrity and even a small bit of wisdom goes a long way to providing you with that critically important resilience factor that might make or break you when the chips are down.

Prophets or poets of each age are given to humanity to help us to awaken from sleep. Those who come back time after time are called Bodhisattvas. They usually end up living ordinary lives of service to others. In their spirit, they have taken vows to return in service to humanity until humanity awakens.

Thus, the path of enlightenment is found in relationship with others who are struggling on the same path within the Earth World, walking in the fog of dim daylight, lost within the deep darkness of night, and in solidarity with those who are bound by a pervasive hopelessness and despair within the World Beneath the Earth. Thus, visions or not, we often learn the hard way.

At least by taking up these skills you will have more resources and more choices when you need them. Over the years we have shared these skills and teachings with hundreds of clients, dozens of therapists who we have supervised, thousands of students, and now with even more readers and interested members of society. The skills and teachings have stood the test of time and are central to forming a strong personal identity, a sense of self, and a basis for growth in personal power, social engagement and relationship wellbeing.

Thank you for taking this journey with me and for reading to this point. I wish you only the best of everything in life, along with peace and true joy in your heart. May you live on the threshold of Manifest Life and through your Life bring Light into the World.

Activity 9 Stardust Awakening

Now, please go back to the beginning of the book and read carefully the spiritual promise that you made to yourself before you began reading into the book. Ponder the text and what this means to you now, compared to then. How have you changed? What new insights have you gained? Does your sense of the text of the promises mean more to you now? Return to your journal, and scribe your awareness and hope for the future…

And find peace in all that remains, for you too are stardust awakening…

www.ingramcontent.com/pod-product-compliance
Lightning Source LLC
Chambersburg PA
CBHW020753020526
44116CB00028B/184